Grade 4

Celebration Press Reading

Good Habits
Great Readers™
Planning Guide

PEARSON

Upper Saddle River, New Jersey
Boston, Massachusetts
Chandler, Arizona
Glenview, Illinois

We wish to thank the following teachers who contributed to the development of the
Celebration Press Reading: Good Habits, Great Readers™ Planning Guides:

Helen S. Comba
K–5 Language Arts Supervisor
School District of the Chathams, NJ

Max Brand
Grade 5 Teacher
Eli Pinney Elementary School
Dublin, OH

The following people have contributed to the development of this product:
Art and Design: Tricia Battipede, Susan Brorein
Editorial: Alia Lesser, Betsy Niles, Jeff Shagawat, Constance Shrier, Shirley White
Instructional Services—Curriculum: Lenore Levy, Roslyn Poole
Inventory: Yvette Higgins
Procurement: Nathan Kinney
Product Management: Alexandra Rivas-Smith
Production Planning and Coordination: Alan Dalgleish, John Rosta
Technical Operations: Larry Berkowitz, Renee Roberts-Chamorro

ISBN-13: 978-1-4284-1914-8
ISBN-10:   1-4284-1914-4

5 6 7 8 9 10 V051 13 12 11 10

PEARSON

1-800-321-3106
www.pearsonschool.com
www.goodhabitsgreatreaders.com

Contents

Overview of *Celebration Press Reading: Good Habits, Great Readers*™ 4

The Reading Program 5

Shared Reading 5

Guided Reading 5

Literacy Centers and Literature Discussion Groups 6

The Writing Program 7

Good Habits, Great Readers **Grade 4 Components** 8

Planning Guide 9

Daily Planner 10

Assessment Materials and Pacing 12

Q&A About Shared Reading 14

Q&A About Guided Reading 16

Q&A About Writing 18

Managing Shared Reading, Guided Reading, and Writing 20

Teachers Share Their Experiences Using *Good Habits, Great Readers* 22

Daily Planners for Unit 1 24

Daily Planners for Unit 2 28

Daily Planners for Unit 3 38

Daily Planners for Unit 4 46

Daily Planners for Unit 5 54

Daily Planners for Unit 6 64

Daily Planners for Unit 7 72

Good Habits, Great Readers™

Celebration Press Reading: Good Habits, Great Readers™ is a comprehensive reading and writing curriculum for Kindergarten through 5th grade. The Reading program supports literacy learning through whole-group (Shared) and small-group (Guided) instruction. In Shared Reading lessons, teachers introduce key reading strategies and skills in a whole-group setting and build a common way of talking about books. During Guided Reading, teachers provide instruction targeted to specific developmental levels. The Writing program provides teachers with an opportunity to model for students the practices, skills, and strategies proficient writers use to express themselves and communicate in a variety of genres.

Good Habits, Great Readers is based on the seven research-based habits and strategies of good readers. It is based on the theory that when good readers read, they utilize specific actions (good habits) to make sense of text, and that teachers can help students learn these good habits. The program's goal is to create both Great Readers and Great Teachers.

Good Habits, Great Readers reflects the work of well-known literacy scholars and incorporates recent research identifying successful literacy strategies and routines, as well as qualities of effective literacy teachers and classrooms. Specifically, the program provides systematic instruction and practice in five domains of reading (phonemic awareness, phonics, fluency, vocabulary, and comprehension) that research shows students must be taught in order to read successfully.

Coordinated with the Reading program, *Good Habits, Great Readers Writing* is designed to help students understand the reading-writing connection and become proficient writers. Through instructional shared and independent writing activities, students are introduced to the writing process and practice the six traits of writing as they write in both fiction and nonfiction genres.

A variety of assessment options are available for *Good Habits, Great Readers* and *Writing*. Informal assessment opportunities are embedded throughout program components, including Shared and Guided Reading lessons and in the Writing units. A four-page Assessment Card provides a framework for ongoing observational and informal assessment in reading, and can be used as a guide for moving students up to the next Guided Reading level. A separate Assessment Handbook for reading provides ready-to-use checklists, recording forms, and surveys to help monitor and assess students' progress in reading throughout the year.

In the Writing program, a Conference Card is provided as a resource for conferring with students. The card contains prompts, reflection questions, and a guide for advising students based on their responses. An Assessment Handbook is found at the back of the Writing Teacher's Guide. It provides information and instruction on using formal and informal assessment to monitor student progress. A variety of writing assessment forms are also available on the Teacher Resource CD.

The *Good Habits, Great Readers* authors are all highly regarded experts in the field of literacy and language education.

Dr. Douglas Fisher is Professor of Literacy and Language Education in the School of Teacher Education at San Diego State University. His writing on the subjects of reading and literacy includes *Reading for Information in Elementary School* (2006).

Dr. Nancy Frey taught in the elementary and middle schools of Broward County, Florida. She is currently Associate Professor of Literacy in the School of Teacher Education at San Diego State University.

Dr. Adria Klein is Professor Emeritus of Reading Education at California State University, San Bernardino and a Visiting Professor at Saint Mary's College. She served as president of the California Reading Association and as a board member of the International Reading Association.

The Reading Program

Shared Reading

Each week of *Celebration Press Reading: Good Habits, Great Readers*™ Shared Reading includes two Mini-lessons and three Focus Lessons. The type and number of lessons varies from day to day. Consequently, daily instructional time varies from 10 to 55 minutes per day. During Shared Reading, the teacher models (using think-alouds) the habits, skills, and strategies proficient readers use to understand and enjoy reading. Each of the seven instructional units covers one of the identified habits of proficient readers, so students learn to:

- See themselves as readers
- Make sense of text
- Use what they know
- Understand how stories work
- Read to learn
- Monitor and organize ideas and information
- Think critically about books

Each Shared Reading Focus Lesson explores a specific comprehension strategy or reading habit tied to the week's strategy. An engaging, developmentally appropriate think-aloud helps the teacher model the strategy. Critical thinking prompts and discussion questions help students apply the modeled strategy and interact with peers to deepen understanding of the content. Once students have learned and practiced a day's focus strategy, they are given the opportunity to apply it, using a text found in the Student Reader. Additional critical thinking prompts and discussion questions, as well as a graphic organizer, help the teacher direct and focus students' thinking and understanding.

Two skill-based Mini-lessons are designed to be incorporated into each instructional week. The flexibility of the Mini-lessons makes them equally appropriate for whole-class or small-group instruction. Mini-lessons focus on five main skill areas: fluency, word study, writer's craft, nonfiction text features, and nonfiction text structure. Mini-lessons provide a brief introduction to a skill or review a skill familiar to students. Each lesson provides opportunities for students to apply the skill, using text from the Student Reader.

Shared Reading lessons include behavior-based prompts and questions to use during conferences to assess students' understanding and ability to apply focus strategies. For a complete list of questions for reading conferences, see the Assessment Handbook, pages 66–73. For students in need of additional help, Shared Reading lessons include opportunities for reteaching and extending lessons, as well as ESL/ELL activities.

Guided Reading

The *Celebration Press Reading: Good Habits, Great Readers*™ Guided Reading lessons are designed to be used with small groups for 20 to 30 minutes to address specific reading skills and strategies. Guided Reading allows teachers to instruct small groups of students with similar learning needs, using a text that is carefully matched to their current instructional needs. Each Guided Reading teaching plan covers two to four days, during which the teacher provides direct instruction in reading skills and strategies and gathers informal assessment information by listening to students read and discuss text.

Before students read, the teacher shares questions and activities to help students activate and use prior knowledge, build background knowledge, make connections and predictions, set a purpose for reading, preview vocabulary, and explore a featured reading skill. As students read independently, the teacher uses prompts that provide support. Finally, after reading, students revisit the featured reading skill and discuss the text. Every lesson plan includes a reproducible that directly extends and/or reinforces one of the reading skills. Assessment Checkpoints help teachers determine if individual students have understood the lesson. A separate section provides optional activities, including an in-depth look at topics not covered in the lesson, a writing activity, a word study mini-lesson, and tips and activities for adapting the lesson for ESL/ELL students.

Literacy Centers

Working independently or in small groups helps students extend and reinforce aspects of reading taught in whole-class or small-group lessons. Teachers can provide these opportunities for students in literacy centers.

Writing activities that may be used in centers can be found in the Guided Reading teaching plans and in the Writing Teacher's Guide. In addition, the Shared Reading Teacher Resource CD provides reproducible pages from select teacher modeling texts, as well as lesson-specific graphic organizers that may be used for independent or small-group work in literacy centers.

Ready-to-use center activities can also be found in programs that complement *Good Habits, Great Readers*, including *Words Their Way*: *Word Study in Action* and *QuickReads®*.

Literature Discussion Groups

Literature discussion groups, also known as book clubs and literature circles, are small, flexible groups of students who meet regularly to read and discuss the same text. These groups provide students with opportunities to explore their understanding of a text while practicing and applying comprehension strategies, building collaborative relationships with classmates, and strengthening communication skills.

In more structured situations, groups meet on a rotating basis, which allows the teacher to facilitate each group. In less-structured groups, the teacher might move from group to group, spending a few minutes with each as students use notes to guide their conversations. As students become more proficient and gain confidence in being a part of a group, they can work more independently. However, the teacher should continue to be involved in a guiding role.

Students usually form groups based on their interest in reading a particular text. Within a discussion group, students may take on certain roles or responsibilities related to reading strategies, such as initiating discussions, making connections, creating visuals, defining vocabulary, analyzing characters, summarizing, and researching background information. These roles are modeled and taught to the group before students fill them independently. Students can rotate roles for each meeting to practice new strategies.

As much as possible, students should be allowed to select books for their groups to encourage their participation and support their growing independence as readers. Teachers can preselect themes and guide students' choices by using book talks to introduce selected titles. Following the book talks, students can mark their preferences on a form. The form should include a list of the book choices for students to number in order of preference and space for the student to record the book title and group members of their last literature discussion group. Of course, other factors may come into play in placing students in groups, including social structures and text difficulty. Preview books and select high-quality titles that represent not only a variety of genres, but also students' culturally diverse world.

Share these tips with students to help promote constructive conversations:

- Ask questions if you need clarification on a statement or idea.

- Be sure to provide evidence that support your idea.

- Request evidence when you disagree with someone's idea.

- Take an idea that is presented and add your own thoughts.

The Writing Program

Celebration Press Reading: Good Habits, Great Readers™ Writing adds a comprehensive Kindergarten through 5th grade writing strand to the reading program. The program can easily be paired with reading and integrated into the daily classroom routine because it supports and extends the strategies taught in the Shared Reading program, and relies on real literature to model writing and highlight techniques used by published authors. During Writing lessons, the teacher works with the whole class to model the practices, skills, and strategies proficient writers use to express themselves and communicate in a variety of genres. Students then work independently or in small groups to reinforce and extend what they've learned.

Like the Shared Reading program, the Writing program is organized into seven units. Each unit focuses on a single genre of writing, for example, narrative writing. Throughout the program, students use the writing process to generate ideas or topics to write about, plan their writing, write drafts, revise, edit, and publish their work. They have frequent opportunities to work together to practice what they've learned and to share their writing.

There are two types of lessons—regular lessons and Trait Time lessons. Regular writing lessons follow the same carefully planned structure, making them easy for teachers to use. The sections of each lesson comprise the three parts of a writing workshop. The Introduce and Teach sections comprise a mini-lesson that provides 10 to 15 minutes of direct instruction. The Introduce section provides context for the lesson, connects the lesson to previous instruction, and names the one main teaching point of the day. In the Teach section, the teacher shows a stage of the writing process or explains how to apply a skill or strategy. This instruction may take the form of modeled writing, shared writing, studying a Shared Reading text or other authentic model, or studying a student-writing model. A form of guided practice follows the instruction. During the Apply section of the lesson, students write and confer with the teacher. During Share, the last section of the lesson or writing workshop, students share their writing in small groups or as a whole class.

There are six Trait Time lessons. The first two regular lessons in Unit 1 introduce the six traits of good writing. Then there is one Trait Time lesson for each trait. In a Trait Time lesson, a trait is defined, an example is provided, and a rubric is introduced for evaluating the trait in a piece of writing. The class works together to use the rubric to evaluate a strong benchmark paper. Students apply what they have learned by working in pairs to evaluate another, weaker benchmark paper and revise it to make it better. The lesson concludes with pairs sharing their work in small groups or with the whole class.

Additional features of the Writing program include Grammar/Usage/Mechanics Mini-lessons and Follow-up Activities, as well as Quick Write and Write to Learn prompts. Quick Write prompts are warm-up or fluency exercises related to the genre students are studying. Write to Learn prompts are for science or social studies content-area writing. Quick Write and Write to Learn prompts can be used in a variety of ways, including before or after writing lessons, as Center Activities, and for independent work. In addition, Conferencing Prompts are provided within the lessons, along with tips for helping English language learners with concepts, content, and vocabulary.

At the end of each unit, students have an opportunity to publish or share their work. Informal Assessment questions help students think about their writing and help teachers assess each student's progress.

Good Habits, Great Readers

Grade 4 Components

For Grade 4, the program includes the following components:

Shared Reading

- 9 teacher modeling texts (3 fiction; 6 nonfiction)
- 3 Student Readers
- 3 audio CDs of Student Reader excerpts
- 1 Teacher Resource CD that contains pages from select teacher modeling texts, graphic organizers, professional articles, and background information on the teacher modeling texts
- 1 spiral-bound Teacher's Guide

Guided Reading

- 45 little book titles, packaged in 6-packs (18 fiction; 27 nonfiction) All 45 books at DRA Level 40
- 1 six-page teaching plan for each little book title

Writing

- 1 Teacher's Guide with embedded Assessment Handbook
- 1 Teacher Resource CD with model texts, sample student writing (benchmark papers), assessment rubrics, graphic organizers, and other support materials
- 1 Conference Card

Reading Assessment Tools

- 1 Assessment Handbook with background information on assessment, along with ready-to-use rubrics, running records, and checklists
- 1 Assessment Card with reading prompts and a checklist to help determine when to move students to the next Guided Reading group

Online Searchable Database

- A full online searchable database of all *Good Habits, Great Readers* Guided Reading teaching plans that users can search by skill, DRA level, book title, and *DRA2* Focus for Instruction
- Access to the Guided Reading teaching plans for the grade above and the grade below to use with struggling readers and students who are reading above grade level

Additional Items for Purchase

- *Skills for Super Writers*
- *Words Their Way: Word Study in Action*
- *DRA2*
- *QuickReads®*

Planning Guide

The *Celebration Press Reading: Good Habits, Great Readers*™ Planning Guide provides teachers with specific guidance on how to integrate all three *Good Habits, Great Readers* programs into their day-to-day instructional routine.

The Planning Guide consists of 28 Daily Planner charts, one for each week of Shared Reading instruction. Each Daily Planner displays the Shared Reading, Guided Reading, and Writing lessons recommended for each day of the week. These recommendations are intended as teaching suggestions for each week's lessons and not as a prescription for what should be taught at a particular time. Teachers can make needed adjustments to the list of recommended activities for a day or the week.

Also included in each Daily Planner chart are Center Activities that can be used in conjunction with Guided Reading, as well as assessment suggestions for Shared Reading, Guided Reading, and Writing. The specific assessment suggestions for each week are based on the Shared Reading, Guided Reading, or Writing lessons and objectives for that week. It is not necessary to use them all. Teachers should choose assessment activities in accordance with their students' needs and district's requirements, and as time permits.

Because the number of Daily Planners is based on the 28 weeks of Shared Reading, and Writing contains 26 weeks of instruction, there are two Writing Catch-up Weeks built into the Planning Guide. Teachers may use the two Writing Catch-up Weeks to have students complete unfinished writing projects or do any of the writing activities listed under Center Activities.

In addition, Writing contains three to four lessons per week, whereas there are five lessons per week in Shared Reading. This means there are one or two days of Flexible Time available each week in Writing. Flexible Time gives students an opportunity to complete their writing projects, focus on an aspect of writing, or do a writing activity listed under Center Activities. Flexible Time also provides opportunities for teachers to confer with students about their writing or to complete any of the assessment suggestions offered in the Daily Planner. The Daily Planners suggest days on which to utilize Flexible Time, but teachers may schedule this time whenever it best meets the needs of their class.

Daily Planner

Each Daily Planner in the Planning Guide gives a day-by-day listing of recommended activities and time frames for a week of Shared Reading, Guided Reading, and Writing.

The number of each Daily Planner is based on Shared Reading. See the Writing band for the corresponding Writing Unit and Week, as they may not always match Shared Reading.

Each Shared Reading unit is based on one of the habits of great readers. Each week explores a featured comprehension strategy or reading habit. Page numbers refer to the corresponding lesson in the Shared Reading Teacher's Guide. The total time covers the Mini-lesson, Focus Lesson, and/or Informal Assessment for each day.

Guided Reading begins in Unit 2. This gives teachers time to establish reading groups in the first few weeks of the program. Recommendations for Guided Reading teaching plans that support the Shared Reading instruction are listed along with Center Activities in the Guided Reading box at the bottom of the page.

Each unit in the Writing program focuses on a genre and one or more modes of writing within the genre. The page references refer to the lesson in the Writing Teacher's Guide.

Week 1 DAILY PLANNER

	Day 1	Day 2
Shared Reading **Unit 2/Week 1**: Great Readers Make Sense of Text/Making Predictions Teacher's Guide, pp. 64–73 Total time: 30–55 minutes per day	Introduce the Teacher Modeling Text: *In the Mountains* 10 minutes Introduce the Student Reader, Vol. 1: *Taste of America* 10 minutes *Mini-lesson* **Nonfiction Text Features** (p. 65) 10 minutes	*Focus Lesson 1* **Activating Prior Knowledge to Make Predictions** (p. 66): *In the Mountains* 25 minutes **Apply the Strategy** (p. 67) **Informal Assessment** (p. 73): **Behaviors to Notice**, bullet 1 **Check for Understanding**, bullet 1 15 minutes
Guided Reading/ *Center Activities* Total time: 60 minutes per day	20–30 minutes for each Guided Reading group 10–20 minutes for each Center Activity	20–30 minutes for each Guided Reading group 10–20 minutes for each Center Activity
Writing * **Unit 1/Week 3**: Descriptive Writing/Descriptive Essay Teacher's Guide, pp. 32–35 Total time: 35–45 minutes per day * Please note that the Writing Unit/Week number is different from the Shared Reading Unit/Week number.	*Lesson 1* **Trait Time—Ideas** (p. 32) 30 minutes **Grammar/Usage/Mechanics Mini-lesson** (p. 146) 15 minutes	*Lesson 2* **Prewriting** (p. 33) **Informal Assessment** (p. 40): **Behaviors to Notice**, bullet 2 35 minutes

Guided Reading

Teaching Plans

These teaching plans support the Shared Reading instruction:

DRA Level 40 *The Ancient Ones: The Anasazi of Mesa Verde; Hurricane; Seeing Is Not Believing*
DRA Level 30 *Koalas; Tigers; The Wonder of Whales*

Center Activities

Have students work independently or in small groups to complete the following activities:

Writing (Guided Reading Teaching Plans, p. 5)

Quick Write (Writing Teacher's Guide, Week 3, p. 25)

Write to Learn (Writing Teacher's Guide, Week 3, p. 25)

***Words Their Way* Connection**
Have students work on *Words Their Way: Word Study in Action* activities.

QuickReads® Connection
Have students read their assigned *QuickReads®* passage.

28   Unit 2 • Week 1

Day **3**	Day **4**	Day **5**
Focus Lesson 2	*Focus Lesson 3*	**Pause and Reflect** (p. 72)
Using Text Structure to Make Predictions (p. 68): *In the Mountains*	**Using Text Features to Make Predictions** (p. 70): *In the Mountains*	15 minutes
25 minutes	25 minutes	**Write About It** (p. 72)
		15 minutes
Apply the Strategy (p. 69)	**Apply the Strategy** (p. 71)	
Informal Assessment (p. 73):	**Informal Assessment** (p. 73):	
Behaviors to Notice, bullet 2	**Behaviors to Notice**, bullet 3	
15 minutes	**Check for Understanding**, bullets 2 & 3	
	15 minutes	
	Mini-lesson	
	Word Study (p. 65)	
	15 minutes	
20–30 minutes for each Guided Reading group	20–30 minutes for each Guided Reading group	20–30 minutes for each Guided Reading group
10–20 minutes for each Center Activity	10–20 minutes for each Center Activity	10–20 minutes for each Center Activity
Lesson 3	*Lesson 4*	**Flexible Time** Use this time to have students work on their writing or to focus on an aspect of writing. You may also confer with students or use one of the assessment materials listed below.
Prewriting (p. 34)	**Drafting** (p. 35)	
Informal Assessment (p. 40):	**Informal Assessment** (p. 40):	
Behaviors to Notice, bullet 3	**Behaviors to Notice**, bullet 7	
30 minutes	35 minutes	
Grammar/Usage/Mechanics Follow-up Activity (p. 41)		
15 minutes		

Depending on the number of Writing lessons for the week, there may be one or two days of Flexible Time.

Recommended assessment tools are listed for Shared Reading, Guided Reading, and Writing.

Assessment

See pages 12–13 to locate the assessment materials listed below. Use the materials during the week based on students' needs and as time permits.

Shared Reading and Guided Reading

- Use the If/then chart in the **Assessment Card** to identify common student problems and provide support.
- Have students use the **Reading Log** to record their reading.
- Use the **Guided Reading Discussion Checklist** to assess students' speaking and listening skills during Guided Reading.

Writing

- Use the **Conference Card** to confer with students.

Assessment Materials and Pacing

Use this chart to locate Assessment materials referenced in the Daily Planners. Also see the Assessment Handbook and the Assessment section of the Writing Teacher's Guide for more information about Shared Reading, Guided Reading, and Writing assessment.

Reading Assessment

Assessment Tool	Location	Purpose	When to Use
Assessment Card	Volume 1 of the Guided Reading teaching plans	Provides a framework for ongoing observational and informal assessment	Ongoing
Summary Rubric	Assessment Handbook, p. 31	Assesses comprehension	Repeat every 2–4 weeks for struggling readers; every 8–10 weeks for readers on or above grade level
Story Frame	Assessment Handbook, p. 33	Supports students' identification of important elements of a fiction selection	Use when introducing summary writing, and with students who need extra support
Text Frame	Assessment Handbook, p. 34	Supports students' identification of important ideas in a nonfiction selection	Use when introducing summary writing, and with students who need extra support
Running Record	Assessment Handbook, p. 39	Assesses comprehension, fluency, and word-solving strategies	Repeat every 2–4 weeks for stuggling readers; every 8–10 weeks for readers on or above grade level
Independent Reading Behaviors Checklist	Assessment Handbook, p. 43	Assesses ability to select, read, and comprehend text independently	Repeat every 8–10 weeks until mastery
Guided Reading Discussion Checklist	Assessment Handbook, p. 45	Assesses speaking and listening skills during Guided Reading	Repeat every 8–10 weeks until mastery
Reading Log	Assessment Handbook, p. 47	Keeps a record of books read	Ongoing
Checklists of Good Habits	Assessment Handbook, pp. 49–55	Assess understanding and use of strategies taught in each Shared Reading unit	End of each Shared Reading unit
Portfolio Selection Slip	Assessment Handbook, p. 58	Helps students self-evaluate items placed in the portfolio	Ongoing
Portfolio Checklist	Assessment Handbook, p. 59	Keeps a record of items placed in the portfolio	Ongoing
Home Reading Record	Assessment Handbook, p. 64	Keeps a record of books read at home	Ongoing
Guided Reading Skills Checklist	Assessment Handbook, p. 74	Keeps a record of skills featured in Guided Reading lesson plans	Ongoing

Writing Assessment

Assessment Tool	Location	Purpose	When to Use
Conference Card	Included with the Writing program	Provides prompts, reflection questions, and a guide to advising students based on their responses	During student writing conferences
Beginning-of-Year Writing Survey	Teacher Resource CD; also see Writing Teacher's Guide, p. 171	Helps students record writing practices and interests and set writing goals	Start of the school year
End-of-Year Writing Survey	Teacher Resource CD; also see Writing Teacher's Guide, p. 171	Helps students reflect on writing accomplishments and set goals for future writing	End of the school year
Conference Record (Individual)	Teacher Resource CD; also see Writing Teacher's Guide, p. 171	Helps teacher record results of individual student conferences, including notes on instructional needs	Ongoing
Conference Record (Class)	Teacher Resource CD; also see Writing Teacher's Guide, p. 171	Provides a record of conference dates with students for each writing unit	Ongoing
My Conference Ideas	Teacher Resource CD; also see Writing Teacher's Guide, p. 172	Helps students record ideas for writing discussed with teacher	Ongoing
Contents of My Portfolio	Teacher Resource CD; also see Writing Teacher's Guide, p. 172	Allows students to record items placed in the portfolio and the dates items were added	Ongoing
Portfolio Selection Slip	Teacher Resource CD; also see Writing Teacher's Guide, p. 172	Helps students reflect on and evaluate items in their portfolio	Ongoing
Teacher Evaluation Checklists	Teacher Resource CD; also see Writing Teacher's Guide, p. 174	Help teacher assess students' writing in a specific genre, use of the six traits of writing, and writing behaviors	End of unit
Anchor Papers and Rubrics	Teacher Resource CD; also see Writing Teacher's Guide, p. 174	Help teacher assess students' writing by comparing finished work to scored samples of students' writing and a rubric	End of unit
Writing Log	Teacher Resource CD; also see Writing Teacher's Guide, p. 175	Provides a cumulative record for students of pieces they have written and what they have learned	Ongoing
Self-Reflection Form	Teacher Resource CD; also see Writing Teacher's Guide, p. 175	Helps students evaluate their writing and reflect on their progress and goals	Ongoing

Q & A About Shared Reading

Q What if my students need more time on one of the Focus Lesson strategies?

A Don't expect that all of your students will get the strategy the first time you model it. These strategies are complex, and the primary purpose of the Focus Lesson is to introduce the strategy. *Celebration Press Reading: Good Habits, Great Readers*™ provides 140 days of classroom instruction, so depending on your school calendar, you will have time to provide additional practice on selected strategies. In addition, you can provide follow-up lessons during your Guided Reading groups.

Each week, the Shared Reading Wrap Up activites reinforce and extend the instruction and learning that have occurred that week. For students who need further support, additional suggestions in the Reteaching and ESL/ELL Support sections help teachers to differentiate instruction.

Q Does *Good Habits, Great Readers* provide instruction for my daily read-alouds?

A Each week, you will be reading aloud text during the Shared Reading lessons. However, you should also make time for additional daily read-alouds. Because your daily read-alouds should ideally be from favorite books (your and/or students' choice) or pieces of shared writing (written collaboratively with your students), you will not find specific lessons for these in *Good Habits, Great Readers*. Read-alouds provide a perfect opportunity for you to include additional think-alouds for your students. Keep in mind the Focus Lesson strategies, and refer to them when appropriate.

Q By the time students reach fourth and fifth grade, they've had several years of instruction on reading strategies. What are the benefits of continuing to teach strategies at the intermediate grades?

A Revisiting key strategies provides opportunities for students to extend their understanding to the more complex text they encounter as they progress through the grades. For example, making predictions becomes a more complex process in the intermediate grades as students need to use a wider range of text features to support reasonable predictions. At the intermediate grades, continuing to teach these comprehension strategies with fiction and nonfiction promotes deeper understanding and encourages success with more challenging text.

Q What is the role of the Mini-lesson in Shared Reading?

A Each Mini-lesson focuses on one of five main skill areas: fluency, word study, writer's craft, nonfiction text features, and nonfiction text structure. There are two skill-based Mini-lessons designed to be incorporated into each instructional week and applied to text from the Student Reader. The flexibility of the lessons makes them appropriate for both whole-class and small-group instruction. Mini-lessons can also be extended and reinforced through the Online Database by searching by skill and the *DRA2* Focus for Instruction. Mini-lessons can be used for instruction in other subjects. Many teachers report great success in incorporating Mini-lessons on nonfiction text features and structures into the content areas.

Q Can I use Guided Reading to reinforce what I've just taught in Shared Reading?

A If assessment embedded in the Shared Reading lessons reveals that students need additional instruction on a particular strategy, you may utilize Guided Reading time to provide this instruction. To assist teachers who wish to make this connection between Shared and Guided Reading, the Daily Planner lists Guided Reading teaching plans that support the Shared Reading instruction. However, it is not recommended that you use your Guided Reading time to only reinforce Shared Reading strategies. The instructional focus of Guided Reading groups should also be based on the results of formative assessments of students' learning needs.

Q I have students who are not reading on grade level. How can I help these students access the text in the Student Readers?

A Teachers have the option of pairing lower-level readers with stronger readers for practicing and applying the strategies. The stronger reader can read the text aloud. Then both students can apply the teacher-modeled strategy. In addition, all of the Student Reader selections are available on an audio CD. Teachers may sometimes work with a small group to address particular needs using the Student Readers.

Q What is the purpose of the Modeling in Action think-aloud in each lesson?

A The Modeling in Action think-aloud is provided in case you need help modeling the strategy. It also helps keep a lesson on target and focused. It is not intended to create a scripted lesson.

Q When is the best time to implement the Apply the Strategy section of the Focus Lesson?

A The Apply the Strategy section is most effective if you implement it soon after you have modeled a strategy for students. You may use this section immediately after the Talk Together section, or you might assign the activity to be done later in the day. Always provide time for whole-class reflection after students work with the Student Reader.

Q How can I be sure that all core reading skills and strategies are covered?

A The program Scope and Sequence can be found in the back of the Shared Reading Teacher's Guide (pp. 354–358). Note the core skills and strategies covered in Grades K–5, which make *Celebration Press Reading: Good Habits, Great Readers*™ a balanced literacy program.

Q & A About Guided Reading

Q **At what point in the school year should I introduce Guided Reading groups?**

A It is recommended that you start Guided Reading groups a few weeks into the year. At that point, you are likely to have formative assessment results that will allow you to tailor instruction to your students' needs. You could start small reading groups prior to this, however, and use these early groups to get to know your students and to teach them effective group behavior and routines.

Q **Do all students participate in Guided Reading lessons?**

A All students can benefit from direct instruction in small Guided Reading groups that meet periodically throughout the year. For struggling readers, Guided Reading is instructionally appropriate for most or all of the school year. Students on or above grade level can meet on a more sporadic basis, balancing time spent in Guided Reading groups with literature discussion groups.

Q **Does Guided Reading always have to follow Shared Reading, as shown in the Daily Planner?**

A The order in which you use Shared and Guided Reading is inconsequential. In addition, the strategies taught in Shared and Guided Reading do not have to be related or correlated. Create a schedule that best fits the class and the needs of your students.

Q **Do I have to do all of the activities included in Guided Reading plans?**

A Some of the activities included in the Guided Reading teaching plans are optional, so you are not expected to do them all. Before students read, it is important to focus their attention, discuss vocabulary, and explore the featured reading skill. As students read independently, you may choose to use the prompts provided, as appropriate. After students read, use the activity that relates to the featured reading skill. Then you can use one or more of the Discuss the Text activities. Choose those that best meet the needs of your students.

Q ***Good Habits, Great Readers* Guided Reading is comprised of books at DRA Level 40 in Grade 4 and DRA Level 50 in Grade 5. How do I use these books with students who are reading above or below grade level?**

A *Good Habits, Great Readers* Guided Reading provides on-grade-level collections for fourth and fifth grades. Students reading above grade level can read more challenging text in literature discussion groups and independently, but for direct instruction of strategies and skills, the text does not have to be at the most difficult level students can manage. *DRA2* recommends that you move students up a level only after they have demonstrated a full range of comprehension strategies in a variety of text types. If you have students who are reading below grade level, you can access appropriate Guided Reading lessons through the online database.

Q What assessments are available for Guided Reading?

A Ongoing assessment is a feature of the Guided Reading lessons. An ideal time to observe students reading and discussing text is in the During Reading section of a lesson. The Assessment Checkpoint section provides prompts for informally assessing students as they read or reread the text. You may also use the Assessment Card and checklists in the Assessment Handbook.

Q How are Guided Reading lessons at the intermediate grades different from those in the primary grades?

A Most of the Guided Reading practices that apply to Grades K–3 also work well for struggling readers in Grades 4–5. For example, intermediate students who are struggling readers benefit from reading aloud, teacher prompting, and direct instruction on decoding and comprehension strategies. For students reading near or above grade level, the procedures may vary a bit. For example, students may read portions of a text silently and then participate in discussion-based work that focuses on comprehension. Because some students in the intermediate grades may read at a fairly high level without fluency, it may be appropriate to incorporate oral reading into lessons to work on expression, pace, and phrasing. At times, a teacher might only read part of a text in a Guided Reading group. For example, he or she might teach the first chapter of a longer text in a Guided Reading group and then confer with students as they complete the book independently or in a literature discussion group.

Q How are Guided Reading groups different from literature discussion groups?

A The main differences between Guided Reading groups and literature discussion groups are the level of teacher involvement and the focus. Guided Reading groups are teacher-directed and focus on specific reading strategies and skills. Literature discussion groups involve more independent work by students. All students benefit from opportunities to participate in literature discussion groups regardless of reading level. This practice strengthens reading stamina and interest and builds supportive social interactions among students. Note that books for Guided Reading are at students' instructional reading level, while books for literature discussion groups are at their independent reading level.

Q Are the books in my *Good Habits, Great Readers* Guided Reading collection also appropriate for literature discussion groups?

A It's best to reserve Guided Reading texts for those carefully structured lessons on specific strategies and skills and to make other choices for literature discussion groups. By bringing other titles into the classroom for literature discussion groups, you'll have opportunities to broaden students' exposure to authors, genres, and topics.

Q & A About Writing

Q How are Writing and Shared Reading connected?

A The Writing program includes 26 weeks of writing instruction that have been mapped to the 28 weeks of *Good Habits, Great Readers* Shared Reading instruction in order to reinforce for students the connection between reading and writing. Structurally, the Writing lessons allow for a gradual release of responsibility from teacher to student, the same as in the Shared Reading lessons. The connections between the strategies of good readers and those of good writers are emphasized throughout the Writing program, and Shared Reading books are often used as writing models. In addition, professional development is embedded in each program. Just as Shared Reading has a Modeling in Action feature, Writing offers modeled "think-alouds," that is, suggested teacher instructional dialogue.

Q Do I have to use *Skills for Super Writers* to get the full benefit from the program?

A How you incorporate grammar into your Writing instruction is completely your decision. Some teachers find that *Skills for Super Writers* is a good resource for teaching skills related to the reading. Other teachers have already planned lessons and resources based on their assessment of students' needs and feel that *Skills for Super Writers* is not necessary.

Q How do the Quick Write and Write to Learn prompts fit into the program?

A Quick Write provides a fluency exercise that often connects to the genre in which students are writing. Write to Learn gives students practice with on-demand writing in social studies or science. Both types of writing prompts can be used at any time and in a variety of ways. You may choose to use them before or after writing lessons, for independent work, as Center Activities, or as homework. You can also create your own writing prompts instead of using the suggested prompts in any unit.

Q Where are the "think-alouds" in the Writing program?

A You will find suggested informal think-alouds in one or two lessons per week. These think-alouds appear in shaded boxes and are found in the Teach portion of the lesson. As you work through the lessons, you will discover that you are asked to model and talk about your thinking about writing in most of the Writing lessons.

Q **Do the Writing lessons have a consistent structure?**

A Although your students may be working on a different stage of the writing process during a particular lesson, you will find that the structure of regular lessons is always the same. The Introduce section provides the teaching point for the lesson; Teach gives the teacher an opportunity to model and then have students practice as a whole group or with partners; Apply is where students write independently; and Share wraps up the lesson with either teacher- or student-directed sharing of the day's work. Trait Time lessons have a slightly different structure in that you define a writing trait, evaluate a benchmark paper with students using a rubric, and then have students examine a second benchmark paper and revise it to improve the trait. The lesson ends with students sharing and discussing their revisions. Both regular lessons and Trait Time lessons are structured to allow for a gradual release of responsibility from the teacher to the student.

Q **When are writing conventions assessed and corrected?**

A Students assess and correct their grammar, spelling, and usage during the Editing step of the writing process. An Editing Checklist and Conventions Rubric can be found on the Writing Teacher Resource CD. Conventions are not assessed when students write in response to a Quick Write or Write to Learn prompt.

Q **How do I assess student writing?**

A An Assessment Handbook is embedded in the Writing Teacher's Guide, which provides support for ongoing assessment, including a variety of assessment tools. In addition, you can use the anchor papers and rubrics, the "What We Notice" charts, and the Conferencing Prompts in each unit's lessons, as well as the Behaviors to Notice and Reflective Writing at the end of each unit to guide your assessment.

Q **Why should I take anecdotal notes as part of assessment?**

A Notes taken while students informally write, and while they use the writing process, provide important information about students' writing. These notes also provide clues to students' understanding of written language. Over time, the notes will allow you insight into students' literacy development.

Q **What if my students need more time to focus on an aspect of writing?**

A There are typically four days of instruction per week, which gives you the flexibility to stretch a lesson over more than one day. Two weeks of catch-up time built into the program allow for additional flexibility. You may also try breaking a lesson into smaller parts, and allowing students to practice between your teaching.

Managing Shared Reading, Guided Reading, and Writing

The goal of *Celebration Press Reading: Good Habits, Great Readers™* is to build a community of readers and writers who are immersed in and excited about becoming proficient readers and writers. Like any community, readers and writers need routines and resources in order to function well. This Planning Guide provides the framework for the time and resources needed to coordinate Shared Reading, Guided Reading, and Writing. In addition, here are some tips for effectively managing Shared Reading lessons, Guided Reading groups, and Writing workshops:

Management Tips for Shared Reading

When introducing and demonstrating the Shared Reading strategy:

- Limit student talk until the Talk Together time.

- Use visuals, such as writing the target strategy, for students to see.

- Keep in mind the Behaviors to Notice while planning and teaching the lesson.

To prepare to model the strategy and use the Modeling in Action:

- Practice the read-aloud and think-aloud and become familiar with the Shared Reading text.

- Find ways to direct students' attention by using highlighting tape and pointers.

During Talk Together:

- Use the suggested activity and questions to deepen students' understanding and to help them apply the strategy.

- Include higher-level open-ended questions in the discussion.

- When grouping students in pairs or small groups, consider needs, interest, social skills, talkativeness, and English-language proficiency.

When the class reviews and reflects:

- Prompt students by occasionally asking them to reflect on and evaluate their participation in the lesson.

When students apply the strategy:

- Scaffold by using the prompts to help students understand how they can independently apply the strategy and use the chart you modeled.

Management Tips for Guided Reading

Before you start:

- Use the reproducible on the back of the teaching plan and photocopy it ahead of time.

When directing students' attention:

- Stay focused and be brief while inviting student participation.

- Refer to what you have noticed about students' reading in order to explain to students why they are in the group.

When introducing vocabulary:

- Use page references to locate vocabulary in context.

- Select key words that are central to the meaning of the text. Other words can be studied in the rereading sections of the lesson.

During reading:

- Focus on one reader while other students silently read the text at their own pace.

- Allow pairs of students seated next to each other to briefly discuss a skill or strategy, if appropriate.

- Avoid stopping the whole group to discuss a point until after reading.

- Take notes, but don't allow note-taking to interfere with observing and interacting with students.

- Engage faster readers by having them reread a selection or a favorite part.

- Encourage readers who are finished early to locate specific information that will be helpful in the after-reading discussion, or have them buddy-reread away from the Guided Reading area to avoid interrupting other students.

After reading:

- Keep notes on observations of specific behaviors that indicate whether students are reading proficiently or having difficulty with the text.

Management Tips for Literacy Centers

- Open one center at a time.

- Keep centers and their management simple.

- Present a mini-lesson that shows how to use the center and explain expectations.

- Invite students to discuss and role-play how to use and share materials, how to take turns, how to solve a problem, where to go for help, how to put things away, and how to switch to another center.

- Allow time for sharing after center work is completed.

- Use a management board that list students' names and where they should be at any given time.

- Keep the groups of students working together at a center small. Sometimes it is best to have only two students at a center.

- Have students change centers every 10 to 20 minutes.

- Create a system for storing completed work, such as individual folders or a central storage place such as a box or tray.

Management Tips for the Writing Workshop

When planning a schedule:

- Use the first weeks of school to let students know what to expect during the three parts of a writing workshop, which are represented by the Introduce and Teach sections; Apply section; and Share section of the lesson. Explain each part, what students will be doing, and for how long.

When setting up a Writing workshop:

- Gather and place needed materials in an easily accessible spot.

- Provide folders, notebooks, and hanging-file folders for students to use as portfolios and to help them organize their work.

- Three-pocket folders can be used throughout the year to keep rubrics, guides, completed and reviewed work, and work in progress.

- Use hanging file folders as portfolios for students to keep representative or favorite pieces of writing, including all related pages for a project (prewriting and notes, rough drafts, and final copy).

- Designate writing notebooks as a tool for students to brainstorm topics, collect details, store memories, record writing tips, and for responding to Quick Write and Write to Learn prompts.

To establish ground rules:

- Emphasize that students should respect one another as writers.

- Prepare a list of behaviors and post them for reference. For example, students should remain quiet during individual writing time.

- Designate a place in the classroom for finished work.

To manage work during the writing process:

- Explain to students that they will be doing short pieces of writing that take a limited amount of time as well as longer pieces that may take several weeks to complete and publish.

- Make sure that students understand what they are to do in each step of the writing process.

- Use provided graphic organizers to help with the prewriting step.

- Recommend that students skip lines and use wide margins in their drafts to allow room for revisions.

- Provide revision suggestions linked to the writing traits and crafts.

- Provide and explain resources for editing.

- Look for publishing ideas in the Unit Wrap Ups.

Good Habits, Great Readers

Helen Comba,
School District of the Chathams, NJ

As our Shared Reading lesson came to an end, I told my students, "Today, we learned how rereading can help us when we are confused about what we are reading. When I meet with you in small groups at the reading table, we are going to work with our little books."

My students know how to move quickly to either Guided Reading or literacy centers. In September, I taught them how to use the schedule that I posted on the wall. Their names are listed next to the title of the leveled reader that they will be reading for the week.

When students are not meeting with me at the reading table, they work on center activities. I don't assign them to work at centers with their Guided Reading groups because I want my students to learn how to work cooperatively and collaboratively with everyone in the class.

My students are able to sign up for the literacy center of their choice each day. The only requirement is that they start at a different center than the one they started with the day before. If they finish an activity, they can return to a center. By the end of the week, students will have had time to work in every center.

Writing is one of the center choices. During this time, students can work on writing that they have in their writing portfolios. This time permits my ELL students to process their thoughts. In between Guided Reading groups, I take time to confer with these or any students who have chosen writing as their center activity.

Of course, not every day is the same. Some days begin with a Quick Write that is related to a mini-lesson or that helps activate background knowledge. At the same time, I am able to confer with students about their independent reading or writing. While it never seems like I have enough time to "do it all," I know that by varying the routine and by differentiating instruction, I will meet the needs of every learner in my classroom.

My Top Five Tips for Managing
Good Habits, Great Readers

1 Scaffold instruction to help students to build independence as readers.

2 Don't ignore the details when practicing routines. Students need to practice how to move around the room, gather materials, and find the right working environment for each activity.

3 Build a sense of community early in the year so that all students work comfortably with one another.

4 Build trust in your students early in the year by teaching them how to make decisions responsibly during independent work time.

5 Allow students to exercise choice. Having choice can motivate students to be more engaged and work successfully on tasks that they enjoy, as well as tasks that they struggle with.

Max Brand,
Eli Pinney Elementary School,
Dublin, OH

I remember early mornings, snuggling close to my mother as her voice brought *The Cat in the Hat* and other Seuss classics to life. Through animated dialogue and discussion, Mom helped me understand how rhythm, rhyme, and repetition are used in texts. Mom's mentoring was my initiation into developing good reading habits. A key tenet of shared reading theory is replicating that early storybook reading experience. The proximity of the participants around a shared text, the dialogue, and the social relationship help novice readers develop the good habits of proficient readers. Now, when I huddle my students around a chart, enlarged text, or common book, this best practice is used to introduce, reinforce, or extend my students' thinking as they develop good reading habits.

The *Good Habits, Great Readers* Teacher's Guides are user-friendly and give me a scope and sequence for teaching my students to be strategic, strong readers and writers. My planning begins by looking at a unit, jotting down areas for instructional emphasis, and then reviewing the weekly focus. I have two and a half hours for daily language arts instruction, and I try to balance the amount of time my kids read and write. Over the course of two-week periods, I try to balance shared experiences with guided reading.

When I preview daily lessons I ask myself: *How will I group the kids so that the lesson will be effective? Which kids should I group together? Will my ELL students fit in well with my less proficient group or should I mix them in with average readers and writers?* The dialogue text boxes help me envision what I will say while interacting with students. For my ELL students, I use the daily lessons in the Teacher's Guides and adjust them so that those children receive more contact with me.

Assessment is important and I try to incorporate it into my daily plans. I try to listen to four to five students read each day. I note their use of reading behaviors taught, using the informal assessment found throughout the program. During writing I try to monitor students' work and read the daily writing of up to five students. I may schedule more time to assess the application of good reading and writing habits of students I'm concerned with.

Experience has taught me that planning ahead is the key to maintaining a well-managed learning environment. These five tips help me keep one step ahead of my learners.

My Top Five Tips for Managing
Good Habits, Great Readers

1 Help students to develop good habits by encouraging sharing, reflection, and discussion in each lesson. Build a sense of community early in the year so that all students work comfortably with one another.

2 Preview the goals for the entire week so that you can guide students toward a weekly goal.

3 Suggested times are just that. Think through how long an activity will take *your* class.

4 Prepare charts before class. As you create each chart, envision the conversation you'll have with students.

5 Enjoy yourself so that your kids will enjoy developing good reading and writing habits.

Week 1 DAILY PLANNER

Shared Reading	Day **1**	Day **2**	
Shared Reading **Unit 1/Week 1**: Great Readers See Themselves as Readers/ Choosing Books Teacher's Guide, pp. 38–47 Total time: 10–45 minutes per day	*Mini-lesson* **Introducing Different Genres** (p. 39) 10 minutes	*Focus Lesson 1* **Having Favorite Books and Authors** (p. 40) 15 minutes **Apply the Strategy** (p. 41) **Informal Assessment** (p. 47): **Behaviors to Notice**, bullet 1 **Check for Understanding**, bullet 1 15 minutes	
Guided Reading/ *Center Activities* There are no Guided Reading groups this week. Guided Reading groups start in Unit 2, Week 1.			
Writing **Unit 1/Week 1**: Descriptive Writing/Getting Started Teacher's Guide, pp. 26–27 Total time: 35 minutes per day	*Lesson 1* **Establish the Writing Workshop in Your Classroom** (p. 26) 35 minutes	*Lesson 2* **Establish the Writing Workshop in Your Classroom** (p. 26) 35 minutes	

Guided Reading

Teaching Plans
There are no Guided Reading teaching plans for this week.

Center Activities
Have students work independently or in small groups to complete the following activities:

Quick Write (Writing Teacher's Guide, Week 1, p. 25)

Write to Learn (Writing Teacher's Guide, Week 1, p. 25)

Words Their Way **Connection**
Have students work on *Words Their Way: Word Study in Action* activities.

QuickReads® **Connection**
Have students read their assigned *QuickReads*® passage.

Day 3	Day 4	Day 5
Focus Lesson 2 **Selecting Books for Independent Reading** (p. 42) 15 minutes **Apply the Strategy** (p. 43) **Informal Assessment** (p. 47): **Behaviors to Notice**, bullet 2 **Check for Understanding**, bullet 2 15 minutes *Mini-lesson* **Protecting Books** (p. 39) 15 minutes	*Focus Lesson 3* **Broadening Your Reading Diet** (p. 44) 15 minutes **Apply the Strategy** (p. 45) **Informal Assessment** (p. 47): **Behaviors to Notice**, bullet 3 **Check for Understanding**, bullet 3 15 minutes	**Pause and Reflect** (p. 46) 15 minutes **Write About It** (p. 46) 15 minutes
Lesson 3 **Establish the Writing Workshop in Your Classroom** (p. 27) 35 minutes	*Lesson 4* **Establish the Writing Workshop in Your Classroom** (p. 27) 35 minutes	**Flexible Time** You may wish to use this time to complete the process of establishing the writing workshop.

Assessment

See pages 12–13 to locate the assessment materials listed below. Use the materials during the week based on students' needs and as time permits.

Shared Reading and Guided Reading

- Have students use the **Reading Log** to record their reading.

Writing

- Have students complete the **Beginning-of-Year Writing Survey**.

	Day 1	Day 2
Shared Reading **Unit 1/Week 2**: Great Readers See Themselves as Readers/ Building Reading Stamina Teacher's Guide, pp. 48–57 Total time: 10–50 minutes per day	*Mini-lesson* **Connecting to Each Other's Ideas** (p. 49) 10 minutes	*Focus Lesson 1* **Building Stamina as Readers** (p. 50) 15 minutes **Apply the Strategy** (p. 51) **Informal Assessment** (p. 57): **Check for Understanding**, bullet 3 15 minutes
Guided Reading/ *Center Activities* There are no Guided Reading groups this week. Guided Reading groups start in Unit 2, Week 1.		
Writing **Unit 1/Week 2**: Descriptive Writing/Descriptive Poem Teacher's Guide, pp. 28–31 Total time: 35–45 minutes per day	*Lesson 1* **Prewriting** (p. 28) 30 minutes **Grammar/Usage Mini-lesson** (p. 146) 15 minutes	*Lesson 2* **Prewriting** (p. 29) **Informal Assessment** (p. 40): **Behaviors to Notice**, bullet 5 35 minutes

Guided Reading

Teaching Plans

There are no Guided Reading teaching plans for this week.

Center Activities

Have students work independently or in small groups to complete the following activities:

Quick Write (Writing Teacher's Guide, Week 2, p. 25)

Write to Learn (Writing Teacher's Guide, Week 2, p. 25)

Words Their Way **Connection**
Have students work on *Words Their Way: Word Study in Action* activities.

QuickReads® **Connection**
Have students read their assigned *QuickReads*® passage.

Day 3	*Day* 4	*Day* 5
Focus Lesson 2 **Setting Long-Term Reading Goals** (p. 52) 15 minutes **Apply the Strategy** (p. 53) **Informal Assessment** (p. 57): **Behaviors to Notice,** bullet 1 **Check for Understanding,** bullet 1 15 minutes	*Focus Lesson 3* **Knowing When Your Comprehension Breaks Down** (p. 54) 25 minutes **Apply the Strategy** (p. 55) **Informal Assessment** (p. 57): **Behaviors to Notice,** bullet 2 **Check for Understanding,** bullet 2 15 minutes *Mini-lesson* **Ask Three Before Me** (p. 49) 10 minutes	**Pause and Reflect** (p. 56) 15 minutes **Write About It** (p. 56) 15 minutes
Lesson 3 **Drafting** (p. 30) 30 minutes **Grammar/Usage Follow-up Activity** (p. 41) 15 minutes	**Flexible Time** Use this time to have students work on their writing or to focus on an aspect of writing. You may also confer with students or use one of the assessment materials listed below.	*Lesson 4* **Revising** (p. 31) **Informal Assessment** (p. 40): **Reflective Writing,** bullet 1 **Behaviors to Notice,** bullet 1 35 minutes

Assessment

See pages 12–13 to locate the assessment materials listed below. Use the materials during the week based on students' needs and as time permits.

Shared Reading and Guided Reading

- Use the **Checklist of Good Habits, Unit 1**, to assess students' understanding of strategies taught.

- Have students select items to add to their reading portfolio and complete the **Portfolio Selection Slip.**
- Have students use the **Reading Log** to record their reading.

Writing

- Use the **Conference Card** as you discuss students' writing with them and offer instructional guidance. Then record your observations on the **Conference**

Record forms, and have students complete the **My Conference Ideas** form.

- Have students add their descriptive poem to their writing portfolio and complete the **Contents of My Portfolio** form and **Portfolio Selection Slip.**

	Day 1	Day 2
Shared Reading **Unit 2/Week 1**: Great Readers Make Sense of Text/Making Predictions Teacher's Guide, pp. 64–73 Total time: 30–55 minutes per day	**Introduce the Teacher Modeling Text:** *In the Mountains* 10 minutes **Introduce the Student Reader, Vol. 1:** *Taste of America* 10 minutes *Mini-lesson* **Nonfiction Text Features** (p. 65) 10 minutes	*Focus Lesson 1* **Activating Prior Knowledge to Make Predictions** (p. 66): *In the Mountains* 25 minutes **Apply the Strategy** (p. 67) **Informal Assessment** (p. 73): **Behaviors to Notice**, bullet 1 **Check for Understanding**, bullet 1 15 minutes
Guided Reading/ *Center Activities* Total time: 60 minutes per day	20–30 minutes for each Guided Reading group 10–20 minutes for each Center Activity	20–30 minutes for each Guided Reading group 10–20 minutes for each Center Activity
Writing * **Unit 1/Week 3**: Descriptive Writing/Descriptive Essay Teacher's Guide, pp. 32–35 Total time: 35–45 minutes per day * Please note that the Writing Unit/Week number is different from the Shared Reading Unit/Week number.	*Lesson 1* **Trait Time—Ideas** (p. 32) 30 minutes **Grammar/Usage/Mechanics Mini-lesson** (p. 146) 15 minutes	*Lesson 2* **Prewriting** (p. 33) **Informal Assessment** (p. 40): **Behaviors to Notice**, bullet 2 35 minutes

Guided Reading

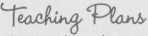

Teaching Plans

These teaching plans support the Shared Reading instruction:

DRA Level 40 *The Ancient Ones: The Anasazi of Mesa Verde; Hurricane; Seeing Is Not Believing*
DRA Level 30 *Koalas; Tigers; The Wonder of Whales*

Center Activities

Have students work independently or in small groups to complete the following activities:

Writing (Guided Reading Teaching Plans, p. 5)
Quick Write (Writing Teacher's Guide, Week 3, p. 25)
Write to Learn (Writing Teacher's Guide, Week 3, p. 25)

***Words Their Way* Connection**
Have students work on *Words Their Way: Word Study in Action* activities.

***QuickReads*® Connection**
Have students read their assigned *QuickReads*® passage.

Day 3	Day 4	Day 5
Focus Lesson 2 **Using Text Structure to Make Predictions** (p. 68): *In the Mountains* 25 minutes **Apply the Strategy** (p. 69) **Informal Assessment** (p. 73): **Behaviors to Notice,** bullet 2 15 minutes	*Focus Lesson 3* **Using Text Features to Make Predictions** (p. 70): *In the Mountains* 25 minutes **Apply the Strategy** (p. 71) **Informal Assessment** (p. 73): **Behaviors to Notice,** bullet 3 **Check for Understanding,** bullets 2 & 3 15 minutes *Mini-lesson* **Word Study** (p. 65) 15 minutes	**Pause and Reflect** (p. 72) 15 minutes **Write About It** (p. 72) 15 minutes
20–30 minutes for each Guided Reading group 10–20 minutes for each Center Activity	20–30 minutes for each Guided Reading group 10–20 minutes for each Center Activity	20–30 minutes for each Guided Reading group 10–20 minutes for each Center Activity
Lesson 3 **Prewriting** (p. 34) **Informal Assessment** (p. 40): **Behaviors to Notice,** bullet 3 30 minutes **Grammar/Usage/Mechanics Follow-up Activity** (p. 41) 15 minutes	*Lesson 4* **Drafting** (p. 35) **Informal Assessment** (p. 40): **Behaviors to Notice,** bullet 7 35 minutes	**Flexible Time** Use this time to have students work on their writing or to focus on an aspect of writing. You may also confer with students or use one of the assessment materials listed below.

Assessment

See pages 12–13 to locate the assessment materials listed below. Use the materials during the week based on students' needs and as time permits.

Shared Reading and Guided Reading

- Use the If/then chart in the **Assessment Card** to identify common student problems and provide support.
- Have students use the **Reading Log** to record their reading.
- Use the **Guided Reading Discussion Checklist** to assess students' speaking and listening skills during Guided Reading.

Writing

- Use the **Conference Card** to confer with students.

	Day 1	Day 2
Shared Reading **Unit 2/Week 2**: Great Readers Make Sense of Text/Asking Questions Teacher's Guide, pp. 74–83 Total time: 20–55 minutes per day	**Introduce the Student Reader, Vol. 1:** *Taste of America* 10 minutes *Mini-lesson* **Nonfiction Text Structures** (p. 75) 10 minutes	*Focus Lesson 1* **Asking Text-Explicit Questions** (p. 76): *Mary on Horseback* 25 minutes **Apply the Strategy** (p. 77) **Informal Assessment** (p. 83): **Behaviors to Notice**, bullet 1 **Check for Understanding**, bullet 1 15 minutes
Guided Reading/ *Center Activities* Total time: 60 minutes per day	20–30 minutes for each Guided Reading group 10–20 minutes for each Center Activity	20–30 minutes for each Guided Reading group 10–20 minutes for each Center Activity
Writing * **Unit 1/Week 4:** Descriptive Writing/Descriptive Essay Teacher's Guide, pp. 36–41 Total time: 35–45 minutes per day * Please note that the Writing Unit/Week number is different from the Shared Reading Unit/Week number.	*Lesson 1* **Drafting** (p. 36) 30 minutes **Grammar/Usage Mini-lesson** (p. 146) 15 minutes	**Flexible Time** Use this time to have students work on their writing or to focus on an aspect of writing. You may also confer with students or use one of the assessment materials listed below.

Guided Reading

Teaching Plans

These teaching plans support the Shared Reading instruction:

DRA Level 40 *Building Bridges; Nutty for Peanuts*
DRA Level 38 *People of the Canyon*
DRA Level 30 *At Home on a Coral Reef*

Center Activities

Have students work independently or in small groups to complete the following activities:

Writing (Guided Reading Teaching Plans, p. 5)
Quick Write (Writing Teacher's Guide, Week 4, p. 25)
Write to Learn (Writing Teacher's Guide, Week 4, p. 25)

***Words Their Way* Connection**
Have students work on *Words Their Way: Word Study in Action* activities.

***QuickReads*® Connection**
Have students read their assigned *QuickReads*® passage.

Day 3	Day 4	Day 5
Focus Lesson 2 **Asking Text-Implicit Questions** (p. 78): *Mary on Horseback* 20 minutes **Apply the Strategy** (p. 79) **Informal Assessment** (p. 83): **Behaviors to Notice,** bullet 2 **Check for Understanding,** bullet 2 15 minutes	*Focus Lesson 3* **Generating Questions Throughout Reading** (p. 80): *Mary on Horseback* 25 minutes **Apply the Strategy** (p. 81) **Informal Assessment** (p. 83): **Behaviors to Notice,** bullet 3 **Check for Understanding,** bullet 3 15 minutes *Mini-lesson* **Fluency** (p. 75) 15 minutes	**Pause and Reflect** (p. 82) 15 minutes **Write About It** (p. 82) 15 minutes
20–30 minutes for each Guided Reading group 10–20 minutes for each Center Activity	20–30 minutes for each Guided Reading group 10–20 minutes for each Center Activity	20–30 minutes for each Guided Reading group 10–20 minutes for each Center Activity
Lesson 2 **Trait Time—Organization** (p. 37) 35 minutes	*Lesson 3* **Revising** (p. 38) **Informal Assessment** (p. 40): **Reflective Writing,** bullet 5 **Behaviors to Notice,** bullets 4 & 6 30 minutes **Grammar/Usage Follow-up Activity** (p. 41) 15 minutes	*Lesson 4* **Editing** (p. 39) **Informal Assessment** (p. 40): **Reflective Writing,** bullets 2–4 35 minutes

Assessment

Shared Reading and Guided Reading

- Use the If/then chart in the **Assessment Card** to identify common student problems and provide support.
- Have students select items to add to their reading portfolio and complete the **Portfolio Selection Slip.**
- Have students use the **Reading Log** to record their reading.

Writing

- Use the **Conference Card** to confer with students.
- Use the **descriptive essay anchor papers** and **rubric** to assess students' descriptive essays.
- Use the **Descriptive Writing Teacher Evaluation Checklist** to track students' acquisition of descriptive writing skills.

- Have students use the **Writing Log** to make a record of completed writing and what they have learned.
- Have students add their descriptive essay to their writing portfolio and complete the **Contents of My Portfolio** form and **Portfolio Selection Slip.**

	Day 1	Day 2
Shared Reading **Unit 2/Week 3**: Great Readers Make Sense of Text/Asking Questions Teacher's Guide, pp. 84–93 Total time: 20–55 minutes per day	**Introduce the Student Reader, Vol. 1:** *Taste of America* 10 minutes *Mini-lesson* **Word Study** (p. 85) 10 minutes	*Focus Lesson 1* **Generating Questions to Anticipate Events or Information** (p. 86): *Mary on Horseback* 25 minutes **Apply the Strategy** (p. 87) **Informal Assessment** (p. 93): **Behaviors to Notice,** bullet 2 **Check for Understanding,** bullet 1 15 minutes
Guided Reading/ *Center Activities* Total time: 60 minutes per day	20–30 minutes for each Guided Reading group 10–20 minutes for each Center Activity	20–30 minutes for each Guided Reading group 10–20 minutes for each Center Activity
Writing * **Unit 2/Week 1:** Narrative Writing/Personal Narrative Teacher's Guide, pp. 42–47 Total time: 35–45 minutes per day * Please note that the Writing Week number is different from the Shared Reading Week number.	*Lesson 1* **Prewriting** (p. 44) **Informal Assessment** (p. 55): **Behaviors to Notice,** bullet 1 30 minutes **Grammar/Usage/Mechanics Mini-lesson** (p. 147) 15 minutes	*Lesson 2* **Prewriting** (p. 45) 35 minutes

Guided Reading

Teaching Plans

DRA Level 40 *Building Bridges; Nutty for Peanuts*
DRA Level 38 *People of the Canyon*
DRA Level 30 *At Home on a Coral Reef*

Center Activities

Writing (Guided Reading Teaching Plans, p. 5)

Quick Write (Writing Teacher's Guide, Week 1, p. 43)

Write to Learn (Writing Teacher's Guide, Week 1, p. 43)

Digging Deeper (Writing Teacher's Guide, Week 1, p. 55)

***Words Their Way* Connection**
Have students work on *Words Their Way: Word Study in Action* activities.

***QuickReads*® Connection**
Have students read their assigned *QuickReads*® passage.

Day 3	Day 4	Day 5
Focus Lesson 2 **Questioning the Author** (p. 88): *Mary on Horseback* 20 minutes **Apply the Strategy** (p. 89) **Informal Assessment** (p. 93): **Behaviors to Notice**, bullet 3 **Check for Understanding**, bullet 2 15 minutes	*Focus Lesson 3* **Asking Questions to Resolve Confusion** (p. 90): *Mary on Horseback* 25 minutes **Apply the Strategy** (p. 91) **Informal Assessment** (p. 93): **Behaviors to Notice**, bullets 1 & 3 **Check for Understanding**, bullets 3 & 4 15 minutes *Mini-lesson* **Fluency** (p. 85) 15 minutes	**Pause and Reflect** (p. 92) 15 minutes **Write About It** (p. 92) 15 minutes
20–30 minutes for each Guided Reading group 10–20 minutes for each Center Activity	20–30 minutes for each Guided Reading group 10–20 minutes for each Center Activity	20–30 minutes for each Guided Reading group 10–20 minutes for each Center Activity
Lesson 3 **Prewriting** (p. 46) **Informal Assessment** (p. 55): **Behaviors to Notice**, bullet 2 30 minutes **Grammar/Usage/Mechanics Follow-up Activity** (p. 55) 15 minutes	*Lesson 4* **Drafting** (p. 47) **Informal Assessment** (p. 55): **Behaviors to Notice**, bullet 4 35 minutes	**Flexible Time** Use this time to have students work on their writing or to focus on an aspect of writing. You may also confer with students or use one of the assessment materials listed below.

Assessment

Shared Reading and Guided Reading

- Use the **Summary Rubric** to assess students' ability to summarize a fiction or nonfiction text.
- Use the **Independent Reading Behaviors Checklist** to assess students' ability to select, read, and comprehend text independently.

- Use the **Running Record** to assess students' comprehension, fluency, and word-solving strategies.
- Use the If/then chart in the **Assessment Card** to identify common student problems and provide support.
- Have students use the **Reading Log** to record their reading.

- Use the **Guided Reading Skills Checklist** to keep a record of skills students have acquired from the Guided Reading lessons.

Writing

- Use the **Conference Card** to confer with students.

	Day 1	Day 2	
Shared Reading **Unit 2/Week 4:** Great Readers Make Sense of Text/Clarifying Teacher's Guide, pp. 94–103 Total time: 20–50 minutes per day	**Introduce the Student Reader, Vol. 1:** *Dancing Around the World* 10 minutes *Mini-lesson* **Writer's Craft** (p. 95) 10 minutes	*Focus Lesson 1* **Using Discussion to Clarify** (p. 96): *Mary on Horseback* 25 minutes **Apply the Strategy** (p. 97) **Informal Assessment** (p. 103): **Behaviors to Notice**, bullet 1 15 minutes	
Guided Reading/ *Center Activities* Total time: 60 minutes per day	20–30 minutes for each Guided Reading group 10–20 minutes for each Center Activity	20–30 minutes for each Guided Reading group 10–20 minutes for each Center Activity	
Writing *** Unit 2/Week 2:** Narrative Writing/Personal Narrative Teacher's Guide, pp. 48–51 Total time: 35–45 minutes per day * Please note that the Writing Week number is different from the Shared Reading Week number.	*Lesson 1* **Trait Time—Voice** (p. 48) 30 minutes **Grammar/Usage Mini-lesson** (p. 147) 15 minutes	*Lesson 2* **Drafting** (p. 49) **Informal Assessment** (p. 55): **Behaviors to Notice**, bullet 3 35 minutes	

Guided Reading

Teaching Plans

DRA Level 40 *Building Bridges; Nutty for Peanuts*
DRA Level 38 *People of the Canyon*
DRA Level 30 *At Home on a Coral Reef*

Center Activities

Writing (Guided Reading Teaching Plans, p. 5)

Quick Write (Writing Teacher's Guide, Week 2, p. 43)

Write to Learn (Writing Teacher's Guide, Week 2, p. 43)

***Words Their Way* Connection**
Have students work on *Words Their Way: Word Study in Action* activities.

***QuickReads*® Connection**
Have students read their assigned *QuickReads*® passage.

Day 3

Focus Lesson 2

Reading Ahead and Rereading to Clarify (p. 98): *Mary on Horseback*
25 minutes

Apply the Strategy (p. 99)
Informal Assessment (p. 103):
Behaviors to Notice, bullet 2
15 minutes

Day 4

Focus Lesson 3

Activating Prior Knowledge to Clarify (p. 100): *Mary on Horseback*
20 minutes

Apply the Strategy (p. 101)
Informal Assessment (p. 103):
Behaviors to Notice, bullets 3 & 4
Check for Understanding,
bullets 1–4
15 minutes

Mini-lesson

Nonfiction Text Features (p. 95)
15 minutes

Day 5

Pause and Reflect (p. 102)
15 minutes

Write About It (p. 102)
15 minutes

20–30 minutes for each Guided Reading group

10–20 minutes for each Center Activity

20–30 minutes for each Guided Reading group

10–20 minutes for each Center Activity

20–30 minutes for each Guided Reading group

10–20 minutes for each Center Activity

Lesson 3

Drafting (p. 50)
30 minutes

Grammar/Usage Follow-up Activity (p. 55)
15 minutes

Lesson 4

Drafting (p. 51)
35 minutes

Flexible Time Use this time to have students work on their writing or to focus on an aspect of writing. You may also confer with students or use one of the assessment materials listed below.

Assessment

Shared Reading and Guided Reading

- Use the If/then chart in the **Assessment Card** to identify common student problems and provide support.
- Have students use the **Reading Log** to record their reading.
- Have students select items to add to their reading portfolio.

- Use the **Portfolio Checklist** to make sure each student's portfolio is organized and up-to-date.

Writing

- Use the **Conference Card** and **conference forms** as you discuss students' writing with them.

	Day 1	Day 2	
Shared Reading **Unit 2/Week 5**: Great Readers Make Sense of Text/Summarizing and Synthesizing Teacher's Guide, pp. 104–113 Total time: 20–55 minutes per day	**Introduce the Student Reader, Vol. 1:** *Dancing Around the World* 10 minutes *Mini-lesson* **Text Structures** (p. 105) 10 minutes	*Focus Lesson 1* **Pausing to Paraphrase as You Read** (p. 106): *In the Mountains* 25 minutes **Apply the Strategy** (p. 107) **Informal Assessment** (p. 113): **Behaviors to Notice,** bullet 1 **Check for Understanding,** bullet 1 15 minutes	
Guided Reading/ *Center Activities* Total time: 60 minutes per day	20–30 minutes for each Guided Reading group 10–20 minutes for each Center Activity	20–30 minutes for each Guided Reading group 10–20 minutes for each Center Activity	
Writing * **Unit 2/Week 3**: Narrative Writing/Personal Narrative Teacher's Guide, pp. 52–55 Total time: 35–45 minutes per day * Please note that the Writing Week number is different from the Shared Reading Week number.	*Lesson 1* **Drafting** (p. 52) **Informal Assessment** (p. 55): **Behaviors to Notice,** bullet 5 30 minutes **Grammar/Usage/Mechanics Mini-lesson** (p. 147) 15 minutes	**Flexible Time** Use this time to have students work on their writing or to focus on an aspect of writing. You may also confer with students or use one of the assessment materials listed below.	

Guided Reading

Teaching Plans

DRA Level 40 *North to the Pole With Matthew Henson; Penguins*
DRA Level 34 *Penguins on Parade*
DRA Level 30 *The Beauty of Bali*

Center Activities

Writing (Guided Reading Teaching Plans, p. 5)

Quick Write (Writing Teacher's Guide, Week 3, p. 43)

Write to Learn (Writing Teacher's Guide, Week 3, p. 43)

Words Their Way **Connection**
Have students work on *Words Their Way: Word Study in Action* activities.

QuickReads® **Connection**
Have students read their assigned *QuickReads®* passage.

Day 3	Day 4	Day 5
Focus Lesson 2 **Distinguishing Between Main Ideas and Details to Create a Summary** (p. 108): *In the Mountains* 25 minutes **Apply the Strategy** (p. 109) **Informal Assessment** (p. 113): **Behaviors to Notice**, bullet 2 **Check for Understanding**, bullet 2 15 minutes	*Focus Lesson 3* **Combining Related Information** (p. 110): *In the Mountains* 25 minutes **Apply the Strategy** (p. 111) **Informal Assessment** (p. 113): **Behaviors to Notice**, bullet 3 **Check for Understanding**, bullet 3 15 minutes *Mini-lesson* **Fluency** (p. 105) 15 minutes	**Pause and Reflect** (p. 112) 15 minutes **Write About It** (p. 112) 15 minutes
20–30 minutes for each Guided Reading group 10–20 minutes for each Center Activity	20–30 minutes for each Guided Reading group 10–20 minutes for each Center Activity	20–30 minutes for each Guided Reading group 10–20 minutes for each Center Activity
Lesson 2 **Revising** (p. 53) 35 minutes	**Flexible Time** Use this time to have students work on their writing or to focus on an aspect of writing. You may also confer with students or use one of the assessment materials listed below.	*Lesson 3* **Editing** (p. 54) **Informal Assessment** (p. 55): **Reflective Writing**, bullets 1–4 30 minutes **Grammar/Usage/Mechanics Follow-up Activity** (p. 55) 15 minutes

Assessment

Shared Reading and Guided Reading

- Use the **Story Frame** or the **Text Frame** and the **Summary Rubric** to assess students' written summaries.
- Use the **Checklist of Good Habits, Unit 2**, to assess students' understanding of strategies taught.
- Use the **Assessment Card** to help determine if students are ready to move to the next reading level.

- Have students use the **Reading Log** to record their reading.

Writing

- Use the **Conference Card** to confer with students.
- Use the **personal narrative anchor papers** and **rubric** to assess students' personal narratives.
- Use the **Narrative Writing Teacher Evaluation Checklist**

to track students' acquisition of narrative writing skills.

- Have students update their **Writing Log**.
- Have students add their personal narrative to their portfolio and complete the **portfolio forms**.
- Have students use the **Self-Reflection Form** to self-assess their writing and to set and evaluate goals.

Week 1 DAILY PLANNER

	Day 1	Day 2
Shared Reading **Unit 3/Week 1:** Great Readers Use What They Know/Activating Background Knowledge Teacher's Guide, pp. 120–129 Total time: 30–45 minutes per day	**Introduce the Teacher Modeling Text:** *The Chocolate Farm* 10 minutes **Introduce the Student Reader, Vol. 1:** *When the Earth Shakes* 10 minutes *Mini-lesson* **Word Study** (p. 121) 10 minutes	*Focus Lesson 1* **Thinking About What You Know Before Reading** (p. 122): *The Chocolate Farm* 25 minutes **Apply the Strategy** (p. 123) **Informal Assessment** (p. 129): **Behaviors to Notice,** bullets 1 & 2 **Check for Understanding,** bullet 1 20 minutes
Guided Reading/ *Center Activities* Total time: 60 minutes per day	20–30 minutes for each Guided Reading group 10–20 minutes for each Center Activity	20–30 minutes for each Guided Reading group 10–20 minutes for each Center Activity
Writing **Unit 3/Week 1:** Response to Reading/Writing to a Prompt Teacher's Guide, pp. 56–61 Total time: 35–45 minutes per day	*Lesson 1* **Prewriting** (p. 58) 30 minutes **Grammar/Usage Mini-lesson** (p. 148) 15 minutes	*Lesson 2* **Prewriting** (p. 59) 35 minutes

Guided Reading

Teaching Plans

DRA Level 40 *The Princess Who Loved to Cook; Robots*
DRA Level 38 *Shark Attack!; Tikky, Tikky Spider*

Center Activities

Writing (Guided Reading Teaching Plans, p. 5)

Quick Write (Writing Teacher's Guide, Week 1, p. 57)

Write to Learn (Writing Teacher's Guide, Week 1, p. 57)

Digging Deeper (Writing Teacher's Guide, Week 1, p. 71)

Words Their Way **Connection**

QuickReads® **Connection**

Day 3	Day 4	Day 5
Focus Lesson 2 **Considering Your Purpose for Reading** (p. 124): *The Chocolate Farm* 15 minutes **Apply the Strategy** (p. 125) **Informal Assessment** (p. 129): **Behaviors to Notice,** bullet 3 **Check for Understanding,** bullet 2 15 minutes	*Focus Lesson 3* **Previewing to Activate Background Knowledge** (p. 126): *The Chocolate Farm* 15 minutes **Apply the Strategy** (p. 127) **Informal Assessment** (p. 129): **Behaviors to Notice,** bullet 4 **Check for Understanding,** bullets 3 & 4 15 minutes *Mini-lesson* **Writer's Craft:** (p. 121) 10 minutes	**Pause and Reflect** (p. 128) 15 minutes **Write About It** (p. 128) 15 minutes
20–30 minutes for each Guided Reading group 10–20 minutes for each Center Activity	20–30 minutes for each Guided Reading group 10–20 minutes for each Center Activity	20–30 minutes for each Guided Reading group 10–20 minutes for each Center Activity
Lesson 3 **Prewriting** (p. 60) 30 minutes **Grammar/Usage Follow-up Activity** (p. 71) 15 minutes	*Lesson 4* **Drafting** (p. 61) **Informal Assessment** (p. 70): **Reflective Writing,** bullets 1, 2, & 5 **Behaviors to Notice,** bullet 3 35 minutes	**Flexible Time** Use this time to have students work on their writing or to focus on an aspect of writing. You may also confer with students or use one of the assessment materials listed below.

Assessment

Shared Reading and Guided Reading

- Use the If/then chart in the **Assessment Card** to identify common student problems and provide support.
- Have students update their **Reading Log.**

Writing

- Use the **Conference Card** and **conference forms** as you discuss students' writing with them.
- Have students add their writing to a prompt to their writing portfolio and complete the **portfolio forms.**

	Day 1	**Day 2**
Shared Reading **Unit 3/Week 2**: Great Readers Use What They Know/Activating Background Knowledge Teacher's Guide, pp. 130–139 Total time: 20–50 minutes per day	**Introduce the Student Reader, Vol. 1:** *When the Earth Shakes* 10 minutes *Mini-lesson* **Writer's Craft** (p. 131) 10 minutes	*Focus Lesson 1* **Activating Background Knowledge Throughout Reading** (p. 132): *The Chocolate Farm* 25 minutes **Apply the Strategy** (p. 133) **Informal Assessment** (p. 139): **Behaviors to Notice**, bullets 1 & 2 **Check for Understanding**, bullet 1 15 minutes
Guided Reading/ *Center Activities* Total time: 60 minutes per day	20–30 minutes for each Guided Reading group 10–20 minutes for each Center Activity	20–30 minutes for each Guided Reading group 10–20 minutes for each Center Activity
Writing **Unit 3/Week 2**: Response to Reading/Summary of Fiction Teacher's Guide, pp. 62–65 Total time: 35–45 minutes per day	*Lesson 1* **Prewriting** (p. 62) 30 minutes **Grammar/Usage/Mechanics Mini-lesson** (p. 148) 15 minutes	*Lesson 2* **Prewriting** (p. 63) 35 minutes

Guided Reading

Teaching Plans

DRA Level 40 *Pockets Full of Gold; Robots; Wacky Weather*
DRA Level 38 *A Home for a Nation; Tikky, Tikky Spider*
DRA Level 30 *Building a Winner*

Center Activities

Writing (Guided Reading Teaching Plans, p. 5)
Quick Write (Writing Teacher's Guide, Week 2, p. 57)
Write to Learn (Writing Teacher's Guide, Week 2, p. 57)
Digging Deeper (Writing Teacher's Guide, Week 2, p. 71)

***Words Their Way* Connection**
***QuickReads*® Connection**

Day **3**	Day **4**	Day **5**
Focus Lesson 2 **Asking Questions to Fill Gaps in Your Background Knowledge** (p. 134): *The Chocolate Farm* 15 minutes **Apply the Strategy** (p. 135) **Informal Assessment** (p. 139): **Behaviors to Notice**, bullet 3 **Check for Understanding**, bullet 2 15 minutes	*Focus Lesson 3* **Revising Background Knowledge to Accommodate New Information** (p. 136): *The Chocolate Farm* 25 minutes **Apply the Strategy** (p. 137) **Informal Assessment** (p. 139): **Behaviors to Notice**, bullet 4 **Check for Understanding**, bullets 3 & 4 15 minutes *Mini-lesson* **Fluency** (p. 131) 10 minutes	**Pause and Reflect** (p. 138) 15 minutes **Write About It** (p. 138) 15 minutes
20–30 minutes for each Guided Reading group **10–20 minutes** for each Center Activity	**20–30 minutes** for each Guided Reading group **10–20 minutes** for each Center Activity	**20–30 minutes** for each Guided Reading group **10–20 minutes** for each Center Activity
Lesson 3 **Drafting** (p. 64) 30 minutes **Grammar/Usage/Mechanics Follow-up Activity** (p. 71) 15 minutes	*Lesson 4* **Drafting** (p. 65) **Informal Assessment** (p. 70) **Reflective Writing**, bullet 4 35 minutes	**Flexible Time** Use this time to have students work on their writing or to focus on an aspect of writing. You may also confer with students or use one of the assessment materials listed below.

Assessment

Shared Reading and Guided Reading

- Use the If/then chart in the **Assessment Card** to identify common student problems and provide support.
- Have students select items to add to their reading portfolio.
- Have students update their **Reading Log**.

- Use the **Guided Reading Skills Checklist** to keep a record of skills students have acquired from the Guided Reading lessons.

Writing

- Use the **Conference Card** to confer with students.
- Have students add their summary of fiction to their writing portfolio and complete the **portfolio forms**.

	Day 1	Day 2
Shared Reading **Unit 3/Week 3**: Great Readers Use What They Know/Making Connections Teacher's Guide, pp. 140–149 Total time: 20–50 minutes per day	**Introduce the Student Reader, Vol. 1**: *Gloria Estefan* 10 minutes *Mini-lesson* **Writer's Craft** (p. 141) 10 minutes	*Focus Lesson 1* **Making Text-to-Self Connections** (p. 142): *The Chocolate Farm* 25 minutes **Apply the Strategy** (p. 143) **Informal Assessment** (p. 149): **Behaviors to Notice**, bullets 1 & 2 **Check for Understanding**, bullet 1 15 minutes
Guided Reading/ *Center Activities* Total time: 60 minutes per day	20–30 minutes for each Guided Reading group 10–20 minutes for each Center Activity	20–30 minutes for each Guided Reading group 10–20 minutes for each Center Activity
Writing **Unit 3/Week 3**: Response to Reading/Summary of Nonfiction Teacher's Guide, pp. 66–71 Total time: 35–45 minutes per day	*Lesson 1* **Prewriting** (p. 66) **Informal Assessment** (p. 70): **Behaviors to Notice**, bullet 2 30 minutes **Grammar/Usage Mini-lesson** (p. 148) 15 minutes	*Lesson 2* **Prewriting** (p. 67) 35 minutes

Guided Reading

Teaching Plans

DRA Level 40 *The Princess Who Loved to Cook; Stop Here! Remarkable Roadside Attractions*
DRA Level 38 *Shark Attack!*

Center Activities

Writing (Guided Reading Teaching Plans, p. 5)

Quick Write (Writing Teacher's Guide, Week 3, p. 57)

Write to Learn (Writing Teacher's Guide, Week 3, p. 57)

Digging Deeper (Writing Teacher's Guide, Week 3, p. 71)

***Words Their Way* Connection**

QuickReads® Connection

Day 3	Day 4	Day 5
Focus Lesson 2 **Making Text-to-Text Connections** (p. 144): *The Chocolate Farm* 15 minutes **Apply the Strategy** (p. 145) **Informal Assessment** (p. 149): **Behaviors to Notice**, bullet 3 **Check for Understanding**, bullet 2 15 minutes	*Focus Lesson 3* **Making Text-to-World Connections** (p. 146): *The Chocolate Farm* 25 minutes **Apply the Strategy** (p. 147) **Informal Assessment** (p. 149): **Behaviors to Notice**, bullets 4 & 5 **Check for Understanding**, bullets 3 & 4 15 minutes *Mini-lesson* **Fluency** (p. 141) 10 minutes	**Pause and Reflect** (p. 148) 15 minutes **Write About It** (p. 148) 15 minutes
20–30 minutes for each Guided Reading group 10–20 minutes for each Center Activity	20–30 minutes for each Guided Reading group 10–20 minutes for each Center Activity	20–30 minutes for each Guided Reading group 10–20 minutes for each Center Activity
Lesson 3 **Drafting** (p. 68) **Informal Assessment** (p. 70): **Behaviors to Notice**, bullet 4 30 minutes **Grammar/Usage Follow-up Activity** (p. 71) 15 minutes	*Lesson 4* **Drafting** (p. 69) **Informal Assessment** (p. 70): **Reflective Writing**, bullets 3 & 4 **Behaviors to Notice**, bullets 1 & 5 35 minutes	**Flexible Time** Use this time to have students work on their writing or to focus on an aspect of writing. You may also confer with students or use one of the assessment materials listed below.

Assessment

Shared Reading and Guided Reading

- Use the If/then chart in the **Assessment Card** to identify common student problems and provide support.
- Have students update their **Reading Log**.

Writing

- Use the **Conference Card** to confer with students.
- Have students add their summary of nonfiction to their writing portfolio and complete the **portfolio forms**.
- Have students update their **Writing Log**.

- Have students use the **Self-Reflection Form** to self-assess their writing and to set and evaluate goals.

	Day 1	Day 2
Shared Reading **Unit 3/Week 4**: Great Readers Use What They Know/Making Inferences Teacher's Guide, pp. 150–159 Total time: 20–45 minutes per day	**Introduce the Student Reader, Vol. 1:** *When the Earth Shakes* 10 minutes *Mini-lesson* **Nonfiction Text Features** (p. 151) 10 minutes	*Focus Lesson 1* **Using What You Know to Make Inferences** (p. 152): *The Chocolate Farm* 20 minutes **Apply the Strategy** (p. 153) **Informal Assessment** (p. 159): **Behaviors to Notice**, bullet 1 **Check for Understanding**, bullet 1 15 minutes
Guided Reading/ *Center Activities* Total time: 60 minutes per day	20–30 minutes for each Guided Reading group 10–20 minutes for each Center Activity	20–30 minutes for each Guided Reading group 10–20 minutes for each Center Activity
Writing **Catch-up Week** You may wish to use this week to have students complete unfinished writing projects or do any of the writing activities listed under *Center Activities.*		

Guided Reading

Teaching Plans

DRA Level 40 *Crossing Borders: Stories of Immigrants; Wacky Weather; What's That Date Again?; What's the Fashion?*
DRA Level 34 *Amphibians; First Kids*
DRA Level 30 *The Great Riddle Mystery; Secrets of the Rainforest*

Center Activities

Writing (Guided Reading Teaching Plans, p. 5)

***Words Their Way* Connection**

***QuickReads*® Connection**

Day 3	Day 4	Day 5
Focus Lesson 2 **Using Inferences to Clarify Words and Concepts** (p. 154): *The Chocolate Farm* 15 minutes **Apply the Strategy** (p. 155) **Informal Assessment** (p. 159): **Behaviors to Notice,** bullet 2 **Check for Understanding,** bullet 2 15 minutes	*Focus Lesson 3* **Revising and Expanding Inferences as You Read** (p. 156): *The Chocolate Farm* 15 minutes **Apply the Strategy** (p. 157) **Informal Assessment** (p. 159): **Behaviors to Notice,** bullet 3 **Check for Understanding,** bullets 3 & 4 15 minutes *Mini-lesson* **Fluency** (p. 151) 15 minutes	**Celebrations** (p. 158) 15 minutes **Write About It** (p. 158) 15 minutes
20–30 minutes for each Guided Reading group **10–20 minutes** for each Center Activity	**20–30 minutes** for each Guided Reading group **10–20 minutes** for each Center Activity	**20–30 minutes** for each Guided Reading group **10–20 minutes** for each Center Activity

Assessment

Shared Reading and Guided Reading

- Use the **Checklist of Good Habits, Unit 3**, to assess students' understanding of strategies taught.
- Use the If/then chart in the **Assessment Card** to identify common student problems and provide support.
- Have students update their **Reading Log**.

- Have students select items to add to their reading portfolio.
- Use the **Portfolio Checklist** to make sure each student's portfolio is organized and up-to-date.
- Review students' **Home Reading Record** to monitor home reading habits and respond to questions or concerns of family members.

- Use the **Guided Reading Skills Checklist** to keep a record of skills students have acquired from the Guided Reading lessons.

Week 1 DAILY PLANNER

	Day **1**	Day **2**	
Shared Reading **Unit 4/Week 1**: Great Readers Understand How Stories Work/ Understanding Story Elements Teacher's Guide, pp. 166–175 Total time: 25–50 minutes per day	**Introduce the Teacher Modeling Text:** *The Renaissance Kids* 10 minutes **Introduce the Student Reader, Vol. 2:** *Spugete* 10 minutes *Mini-lesson* **Word Study** (p. 167) 10 minutes	*Focus Lesson 1* **Previewing a Text** (p. 168): *The Renaissance Kids* 15 minutes **Apply the Strategy** (p. 169) **Informal Assessment** (p. 175): **Behaviors to Notice,** bullet 1 **Check for Understanding,** bullet 1 25 minutes	
Guided Reading/ *Center Activities* Total time: 60 minutes per day	20–30 minutes for each Guided Reading group 10–20 minutes for each Center Activity	20–30 minutes for each Guided Reading group 10–20 minutes for each Center Activity	
Writing **Unit 4/Week 1:** Creative Writing/ Character Sketch Teacher's Guide, pp. 72–77 Total time: 35–45 minutes per day	*Lesson 1* **Prewriting** (p. 74) 30 minutes **Grammar/Usage/Mechanics Mini-lesson** (p. 149) 15 minutes	*Lesson 2* **Prewriting** (p. 75) 35 minutes	

Guided Reading

Teaching Plans

DRA Level 40 *The Mystery of the Hidden Letter; Pockets Full of Gold; Spugete Detectives; The Story of Persephone*
DRA Level 38 *A Home for a New Nation; How Mother Nature Got Her Job; Too Close to the Sun*
DRA Level 30 *Aladdin and the Magic Lamp*

Center Activities

Writing (Guided Reading Teaching Plans, p. 5)

Quick Write (Writing Teacher's Guide, Week 1, p. 73)

Write to Learn (Writing Teacher's Guide, Week 1, p. 73)

Digging Deeper (Writing Teacher's Guide, Week 1, p. 89)

Words Their Way **Connection**
QuickReads® **Connection**

Day 3	Day 4	Day 5
Focus Lesson 2 **Identifying Story Elements** (p. 170): *The Renaissance Kids* 15 minutes **Apply the Strategy** (p. 171) **Informal Assessment** (p. 175): **Behaviors to Notice**, bullet 2 **Check for Understanding**, bullet 2 25 minutes	*Focus Lesson 3* **Identifying Point of View** (p. 172): *The Renaissance Kids* 15 minutes **Apply the Strategy** (p. 173) **Informal Assessment** (p. 175): **Behaviors to Notice**, bullets 3 & 4 **Check for Understanding**, bullets 3 & 4 25 minutes *Mini-lesson* **Writer's Craft** (p. 167) 10 minutes	**Pause and Reflect** (p. 174) 15 minutes **Write About It** (p. 174) 15 minutes
20–30 minutes for each Guided Reading group 10–20 minutes for each Center Activity	20–30 minutes for each Guided Reading group 10–20 minutes for each Center Activity	20–30 minutes for each Guided Reading group 10–20 minutes for each Center Activity
Lesson 3 **Drafting** (p. 76) 30 minutes **Grammar/Usage/Mechanics Follow-up Activity** (p. 89) 15 minutes	**Flexible Time** Use this time to have students work on their writing or to focus on an aspect of writing. You may also confer with students or use one of the assessment materials listed below.	*Lesson 4* **Revising** (p. 77) **Informal Assessment** (p. 89): **Reflective Writing**, bullet 1 **Behaviors to Notice**, bullet 2 35 minutes

Assessment

Shared Reading and Guided Reading

- Use the If/then chart in the **Assessment Card** to identify common student problems and provide support.
- Have students update their **Reading Log**.
- Use the **Guided Reading Discussion Checklist** to assess students' speaking and listening skills during Guided Reading.

Writing

- Use the **Conference Card** and **conference forms** as you discuss students' writing with them.
- Have students add their character sketch to their writing portfolio and complete the **portfolio forms**.

	Day **1**	Day **2**
Shared Reading **Unit 4/Week 2**: **Great Readers Understand How Stories Work/ Understanding and Analyzing Characters** Teacher's Guide, pp. 176–185 Total time: 20–50 minutes per day	**Introduce the Student Reader, Vol. 2:** *Spugete* 10 minutes *Mini-lesson* **Writer's Craft** (p. 177) 10 minutes	*Focus Lesson 1* **Understanding a Character's Purpose** (p. 178): *The Renaissance Kids* 15 minutes **Apply the Strategy** (p. 179) **Informal Assessment** (p. 185): **Behaviors to Notice,** bullets 1 & 2 **Check for Understanding,** bullets 1 & 2 25 minutes
Guided Reading/ *Center Activities* Total time: 60 minutes per day	20–30 minutes for each Guided Reading group 10–20 minutes for each Center Activity	20–30 minutes for each Guided Reading group 10–20 minutes for each Center Activity
Writing **Unit 4/Week 2**: **Creative Writing/Realistic Short Story** Teacher's Guide, pp. 78–81 Total time: 35–45 minutes per day	*Lesson 1* **Prewriting** (p. 78) 30 minutes **Grammar/Usage Mini-lesson** (p. 149) 15 minutes	*Lesson 2* **Prewriting** (p. 79) 35 minutes

Guided Reading

Teaching Plans

DRA Level 40 *Dragon for Sale; Louise Goes to the City; The Otherwhere Ice Show; Taking Care; Trading Places in Timbuktu: A Tale from Mali*
DRA Level 38 *How Mother Nature Got Her Job; It's a Mammal*
DRA Level 34 *Intergalactic Cell Phone*
DRA Level 30 *Grasslands; King Midas and the Golden Touch*

Center Activities

Writing (Guided Reading Teaching Plans, p. 5)

Quick Write (Writing Teacher's Guide, Week 2, p. 73)

Write to Learn (Writing Teacher's Guide, Week 2, p. 73)

***Words Their Way* Connection**

QuickReads® **Connection**

Day 3	Day 4	Day 5
Focus Lesson 2 **Analyzing a Character's Dialogue and Actions** (p. 180): *The Renaissance Kids* 15 minutes **Apply the Strategy** (p. 181) **Informal Assessment** (p. 185): **Behaviors to Notice,** bullet 3 **Check for Understanding,** bullet 3 25 minutes	*Focus Lesson 3* **Understanding How Characters Develop** (p. 182): *The Renaissance Kids* 15 minutes **Apply the Strategy** (p. 183) **Informal Assessment** (p. 185): **Behaviors to Notice,** bullet 4 **Check for Understanding,** bullets 4 & 5 25 minutes *Mini-lesson* **Word Study** (p. 177) 10 minutes	**Pause and Reflect** (p. 184) 15 minutes **Write About It** (p. 184) 15 minutes
20–30 minutes for each Guided Reading group 10–20 minutes for each Center Activity	20–30 minutes for each Guided Reading group 10–20 minutes for each Center Activity	20–30 minutes for each Guided Reading group 10–20 minutes for each Center Activity
Lesson 3 **Prewriting** (p. 80) 30 minutes **Grammar/Usage Follow-up Activity** (p. 89) 15 minutes	*Lesson 4* **Prewriting** (p. 81) **Informal Assessment** (p. 89): **Behaviors to Notice,** bullets 1 & 3 35 minutes	**Flexible Time** Use this time to have students work on their writing or to focus on an aspect of writing. You may also confer with students or use one of the assessment materials listed below.

Assessment

Shared Reading and Guided Reading

- Use the **Summary Rubric** to assess students' ability to summarize a fiction or nonfiction text.
- Use the **Running Record** to assess students' comprehension, fluency, and word-solving strategies.
- Use the If/then chart in the **Assessment Card** to identify common student problems and provide support.

- Have students select items to add to their reading portfolio.
- Have students update their **Reading Log.**
- Use the **Guided Reading Skills Checklist** to keep a record of skills students have acquired from the Guided Reading lessons.

Writing

- Use the **Conference Card** to confer with students.

	Day 1	Day 2
Shared Reading **Unit 4/Week 3**: Great Readers Understand How Stories Work/ Understanding Setting and Plot Teacher's Guide, pp. 186–195 Total time: 20–40 minutes per day	**Introduce the Student Reader, Vol. 2**: *Spugete* 10 minutes *Mini-lesson* **Writer's Craft** (p. 187) 10 minutes	*Focus Lesson 1* **Identifying the Setting** (p. 188): *The Renaissance Kids* 25 minutes **Apply the Strategy** (p. 189) **Informal Assessment** (p. 195): **Behaviors to Notice**, bullet 1 **Check for Understanding**, bullet 1 15 minutes
Guided Reading/ *Center Activities* Total time: 60 minutes per day	20–30 minutes for each Guided Reading group 10–20 minutes for each Center Activity	20–30 minutes for each Guided Reading group 10–20 minutes for each Center Activity
Writing **Unit 4/Week 3**: Creative Writing/Realistic Short Story Teacher's Guide, pp. 82–85 Total time: 35–45 minutes per day	*Lesson 1* **Trait Time—Word Choice** (p. 82) 30 minutes **Grammar/Usage/Mechanics Mini-lesson** (p. 149) 15 minutes	*Lesson 2* **Drafting** (p. 83) 35 minutes

Guided Reading

Teaching Plans

DRA Level 40 *Dragon for Sale; Green Treasure; Kids in Charge; Louisa, the Blind Kitten; Spugete Detectives*
DRA Level 34 *The Go-Boat; Hooray for Rhody!; The Legend of the Blue Bonnets; The Mystery of the Spy's Diary; What Happens to the Dog?*

Center Activities

Writing (Guided Reading Teaching Plans, p. 5)
Quick Write (Writing Teacher's Guide, Week 3, p. 73)
Write to Learn (Writing Teacher's Guide, Week 3, p. 73)

***Words Their Way* Connection**
QuickReads® **Connection**

Day **3**	Day **4**	Day **5**
Focus Lesson 2 **Exploring Relationships Between Setting and Characters** (p. 190): *The Renaissance Kids* 25 minutes **Apply the Strategy** (p. 191) **Informal Assessment** (p. 195): **Behaviors to Notice**, bullet 2 **Check for Understanding**, bullet 2 15 minutes	*Focus Lesson 3* **Identifying and Keeping Track of the Plot** (p. 192): *The Renaissance Kids* 15 minutes **Apply the Strategy** (p. 193) **Informal Assessment** (p. 195): **Behaviors to Notice**, bullet 3 **Check for Understanding,** bullets 3 & 4 15 minutes *Mini-lesson* **Fluency** (p. 187) 10 minutes	**Pause and Reflect** (p. 194) 15 minutes **Write About It** (p. 194) 15 minutes
20–30 minutes for each Guided Reading group 10–20 minutes for each Center Activity	20–30 minutes for each Guided Reading group 10–20 minutes for each Center Activity	20–30 minutes for each Guided Reading group 10–20 minutes for each Center Activity
Lesson 3 **Drafting** (p. 84) **Informal Assessment** (p. 89): **Behaviors to Notice**, bullet 5 30 minutes **Grammar/Usage/Mechanics Follow-up Activity** (p. 89) 15 minutes	**Flexible Time** Use this time to have students work on their writing or to focus on an aspect of writing. You may also confer with students or use one of the assessment materials listed below.	*Lesson 4* **Drafting** (p. 85) **Informal Assessment** (p. 89): **Behaviors to Notice**, bullet 4 35 minutes

Assessment

Shared Reading and Guided Reading

- Use the **Independent Reading Behaviors Checklist** to assess students' ability to select, read, and comprehend text independently.
- Use the If/then chart in the **Assessment Card** to identify common student problems and provide support.

- Have students update their **Reading Log**.
- Use the **Portfolio Checklist** to make sure each student's portfolio is organized and up-to-date.
- Review students' **Home Reading Record** to monitor home reading habits and respond to questions or concerns of family members.

Writing

- Use the **Conference Card** to confer with students.

	Day 1	Day 2	
Shared Reading **Unit 4/Week 4:** Great Readers Understand How Stories Work/ Understanding and Analyzing Theme Teacher's Guide, pp. 196–205 Total time: 20–40 minutes per day	Introduce the Student Reader, **Vol. 2:** *Spugete* 10 minutes *Mini-lesson* **Fluency** (p. 197) 10 minutes	*Focus Lesson 1* **Relating to Characters and Events** (p. 198): *The Renaissance Kids* 15 minutes **Apply the Strategy** (p. 199) **Informal Assessment** (p. 205): **Behaviors to Notice,** bullet 1 **Check for Understanding,** bullet 1 15 minutes	
Guided Reading/ *Center Activities* Total time: 60 minutes per day	20–30 minutes for each Guided Reading group 10–20 minutes for each Center Activity	20–30 minutes for each Guided Reading group 10–20 minutes for each Center Activity	
Writing **Unit 4/Week 4:** Creative Writing/Realistic Short Story Teacher's Guide, pp. 86–89 Total time: 35–45 minutes per day	*Lesson 1* **Revising** (p. 86) 30 minutes **Grammar/Usage Mini-lesson** (p. 149) 15 minutes	**Flexible Time** Use this time to have students work on their writing or to focus on an aspect of writing. You may also confer with students or use one of the assessment materials listed below.	

Guided Reading

Teaching Plans

DRA Level 40 *The Otherwhere Ice Show; Pockets Full of Gold*
DRA Level 38 *A Home for a New Nation*
DRA Level 30 *King Midas and the Golden Touch*

Center Activities

Writing (Guided Reading Teaching Plans, p. 5)

Quick Write (Writing Teacher's Guide, Week 4, p. 73)

Write to Learn (Writing Teacher's Guide, Week 4, p. 73)

Digging Deeper (Writing Teacher's Guide, Week 4, p. 89)

Words Their Way **Connection**

QuickReads® **Connection**

Day 3	Day 4	Day 5
Focus Lesson 2 **Identifying the Theme** (p. 200): *The Renaissance Kids* 15 minutes **Apply the Strategy** (p. 201) **Informal Assessment** (p. 205): **Behaviors to Notice,** bullet 2 **Check for Understanding,** bullet 2 15 minutes	*Focus Lesson 3* **Relating to the Theme** (p. 202): *The Renaissance Kids* 15 minutes **Apply the Strategy** (p. 203) **Informal Assessment** (p. 205): **Behaviors to Notice,** bullet 3 **Check for Understanding,** bullets 3 & 4 15 minutes *Mini-lesson* **Writer's Craft** (p. 197) 10 minutes	**Celebrations** (p. 204) 15 minutes **Write About It** (p. 204) 15 minutes
20–30 minutes for each Guided Reading group **10–20 minutes** for each Center Activity	**20–30 minutes** for each Guided Reading group **10–20 minutes** for each Center Activity	**20–30 minutes** for each Guided Reading group **10–20 minutes** for each Center Activity
Lesson 2 **Revising** (p. 87) **Informal Assessment** (p. 89): **Reflective Writing,** bullet 5 35 minutes	**Flexible Time** Use this time to have students work on their writing or to focus on an aspect of writing. You may also confer with students or use one of the assessment materials listed below.	*Lesson 3* **Editing** (p. 88) **Informal Assessment** (p. 89): **Reflective Writing,** bullets 2–4 30 minutes **Grammar/Usage Follow-up Activity** (p. 89) 15 minutes

Assessment

Shared Reading and Guided Reading

- Use the **Checklist of Good Habits, Unit 4,** to assess students' understanding of strategies taught.
- Use the **Assessment Card** to help determine if students are ready to move to the next reading level.
- Have students select items to add to their reading portfolio.

- Have students update their **Reading Log.**

Writing

- Use the **Conference Card** to confer with students.
- Use the **short story anchor papers** and **rubric** to assess students' realistic short stories.
- Use the **Creative Writing Teacher Evaluation Checklist** to track students' acquisition of creative writing skills.
- Have students add their realistic short story to their writing portfolio and complete the **portfolio forms.**
- Have students update their **Writing Log.**
- Have students use the **Self-Reflection Form** to self-assess their writing and to set and evaluate goals.

	Day 1	Day 2
Shared Reading **Unit 5/Week 1**: Great Readers Read to Learn/Locating Facts and Information Teacher's Guide, pp. 212–221 Total time: 30–50 minutes per day	**Introduce the Teacher Modeling Text**: *Drums: The World's Heartbeat* 10 minutes **Introduce the Student Reader, Vol. 2**: *Skeletons Inside and Out* 10 minutes *Mini-lesson* **Writer's Craft** (p. 213) 10 minutes	*Focus Lesson 1* **Predicting Information Based on the Cover and Contents Page** (p. 214): *Drums: The World's Heartbeat* 25 minutes **Apply the Strategy** (p. 215) **Informal Assessment** (p. 221): **Behaviors to Notice**, bullet 1 **Check for Understanding**, bullet 1 15 minutes
Guided Reading/ *Center Activities* Total time: 60 minutes per day	20–30 minutes for each Guided Reading group 10–20 minutes for each Center Activity	20–30 minutes for each Guided Reading group 10–20 minutes for each Center Activity
Writing **Unit 5/Week 1**: Informational Writing/Interview Teacher's Guide, pp. 90–95 Total time: 35–45 minutes per day	*Lesson 1* **Prewriting** (p. 92) 30 minutes **Grammar/Usage/Mechanics Mini-lesson** (p. 150) 15 minutes	*Lesson 2* **Drafting** (p. 93) **Informal Assessment** (p. 111): **Reflective Writing**, bullet 1 **Behaviors to Notice**, bullet 2 35 minutes

Guided Reading

Teaching Plans

DRA Level 40 *African American Cowboys: True Heroes of the Old West; The Guitar: King of Strings; The Living Desert; Maya Lin: Linking People and Places; Nature's Mysteries*
DRA Level 38 *Chasing Tornados; Encyclopedia of World Sports; They Changed the World; A Year in Antarctica*
DRA Level 30 *Tigers*

Center Activities

Writing (Guided Reading Teaching Plans, p. 5)

Quick Write (Writing Teacher's Guide, Week 1, p. 91)

Write to Learn (Writing Teacher's Guide, Week 1, p. 91)

***Words Their Way* Connection**

QuickReads® **Connection**

Day 3	*Day* 4	*Day* 5
Focus Lesson 2 **Locating Information Using Boldfaced Words and a Glossary** (p. 216): *Drums: The World's Heartbeat* 25 minutes **Apply the Strategy** (p. 217) **Informal Assessment** (p. 221): **Behaviors to Notice**, bullet 2 **Check for Understanding**, bullet 2 15 minutes	*Focus Lesson 3* **Identifying Facts From the Text** (p. 218): *Drums: The World's Heartbeat* 25 minutes **Apply the Strategy** (p. 219) **Informal Assessment** (p. 221): **Behaviors to Notice**, bullet 3 **Check for Understanding**, bullets 3 & 4 15 minutes *Mini-lesson* **Word Study** (p. 213) 10 minutes	**Pause and Reflect** (p. 220) 15 minutes **Write About It** (p. 220) 15 minutes
20–30 minutes for each Guided Reading group 10–20 minutes for each Center Activity	20–30 minutes for each Guided Reading group 10–20 minutes for each Center Activity	20–30 minutes for each Guided Reading group 10–20 minutes for each Center Activity
Flexible Time Use this time to have students work on their writing or to focus on an aspect of writing. You may also confer with students or use one of the assessment materials listed below.	*Lesson 3* **Drafting** (p. 94) 30 minutes **Grammar/Usage/Mechanics Follow-up Activity** (p. 111) 15 minutes	*Lesson 4* **Revising** (p. 95) 35 minutes

Assessment

Shared Reading and Guided Reading

- Use the If/then chart in the **Assessment Card** to identify common student problems and provide support.
- Have students update their **Reading Log**.
- Use the **Guided Reading Skills Checklist** to keep a record of skills students have acquired from the Guided Reading lessons.

Writing

- Use the **Conference Card** to confer with students.
- Have students add their interview to their writing portfolio and complete the **portfolio forms**.

	Day 1	**Day 2**	
Shared Reading **Unit 5/Week 2**: Great Readers Read to Learn/Making Inferences From Nonfiction Teacher's Guide, pp. 222–231 Total time: 20–50 minutes per day	**Introduce the Student Reader, Vol. 2**: *Skeletons Inside and Out* 10 minutes *Mini-lesson* **Nonfiction Text Features** (p. 223) 10 minutes	*Focus Lesson 1* **Developing Inferences From a Stated Fact** (p. 224): *Drums: The World's Heartbeat* 25 minutes **Apply the Strategy** (p. 225) **Informal Assessment** (p. 231): **Behaviors to Notice**, bullet 1 **Check for Understanding**, bullet 1 15 minutes	
Guided Reading/ *Center Activities* Total time: 60 minutes per day	20–30 minutes for each Guided Reading group 10–20 minutes for each Center Activity	20–30 minutes for each Guided Reading group 10–20 minutes for each Center Activity	
Writing **Unit 5/Week 2**: Informational Writing/Taking Notes on Nonfiction Teacher's Guide, pp. 96–99 Total time: 35–45 minutes per day	*Lesson 1* **Prewriting** (p. 96) 30 minutes **Grammar/Usage Mini-lesson** (p. 150) 15 minutes	*Lesson 2* **Prewriting** (p. 97) 35 minutes	

Guided Reading

Teaching Plans

DRA Level 40 *Crossing Borders: Stories of Immigrants; Wacky Weather; What's That Date Again?; What's the Fashion?*
DRA Level 38 *The Creature Vanishes*
DRA Level 34 *Amphibians*
DRA Level 30 *Building a Winner; Secrets of the Rainforest*

Center Activities

Writing (Guided Reading Teaching Plans, p. 5)
Quick Write (Writing Teacher's Guide, Week 2, p. 91)
Write to Learn (Writing Teacher's Guide, Week 2, p. 91)

***Words Their Way* Connection**
QuickReads® **Connection**

Day 3	Day 4	Day 5
Focus Lesson 2 **Using Prior Knowledge to Make Inferences** (p. 226): *Drums: The World's Heartbeat* 25 minutes **Apply the Strategy** (p. 227) **Informal Assessment** (p. 231): **Behaviors to Notice**, bullet 2 **Check for Understanding**, bullet 2 15 minutes	*Focus Lesson 3* **Evaluating Your Inferences** (p. 228): *Drums: The World's Heartbeat* 25 minutes **Apply the Strategy** (p. 229) **Informal Assessment** (p. 231): **Behaviors to Notice**, bullet 3 **Check for Understanding**, bullets 3 & 4 15 minutes *Mini-lesson* **Nonfiction Text Structure** (p. 223) 10 minutes	**Pause and Reflect** (p. 230) 15 minutes **Write About It** (p. 230) 15 minutes
20–30 minutes for each Guided Reading group 10–20 minutes for each Center Activity	20–30 minutes for each Guided Reading group 10–20 minutes for each Center Activity	20–30 minutes for each Guided Reading group 10–20 minutes for each Center Activity
Flexible Time Use this time to have students work on their writing or to focus on an aspect of writing. You may also confer with students or use one of the assessment materials listed below.	*Lesson 3* **Prewriting** (p. 98) 30 minutes **Grammar/Usage Follow-up Activity** (p. 111) 15 minutes	*Lesson 4* **Prewriting** (p. 99) 35 minutes

Assessment

Shared Reading and Guided Reading

- Use the If/then chart in the **Assessment Card** to identify common student problems and provide support.
- Have students select items to add to their reading portfolio.
- Have students update their **Reading Log**.

Writing

- Use the **Conference Card** to confer with students.
- Have students add their notes on nonfiction to their writing portfolio and complete the **portfolio forms**.

	Day 1	Day 2	
Shared Reading **Unit 5/Week 3**: Great Readers Read to Learn/Identifying and Using Text Features Teacher's Guide, pp. 232–241 Total time: 20–50 minutes per day	**Introduce the Student Reader, Vol. 2**: *Skeletons Inside and Out* 10 minutes *Mini-lesson* **Word Study** (p. 233) 10 minutes	*Focus Lesson 1* **Identifying Facts From Visual Sources** (p. 234): *Drums: The World's Heartbeat* 25 minutes **Apply the Strategy** (p. 235) **Informal Assessment** (p. 241): **Behaviors to Notice**, bullet 1 **Check for Understanding**, bullet 1 15 minutes	
Guided Reading/ *Center Activities* Total time: 60 minutes per day	20–30 minutes for each Guided Reading group 10–20 minutes for each Center Activity	20–30 minutes for each Guided Reading group 10–20 minutes for each Center Activity	
Writing **Unit 5/Week 3**: Informational Writing/Science Report Teacher's Guide, pp. 100–103 Total time: 35–45 minutes per day	*Lesson 1* **Prewriting** (p. 100) **Informal Assessment** (p. 111): **Behaviors to Notice**, bullet 1 30 minutes **Grammar/Usage Mini-lesson** (p. 150) 15 minutes	*Lesson 2* **Prewriting** (p. 101) 35 minutes	

Guided Reading

Teaching Plans

DRA Level 40 *Coral Reefs; A Guide to Rocks and Minerals; Hurricane; Nature's Mysteries; Seeing Is Not Believing*
DRA Level 38 *Ellen Ochoa: Reaching for the Stars; Encyclopedia of World Sports*

DRA Level 34 *Away We Go!*
DRA Level 30 *Animals of the Tundra; The Wonder of Whales*

Center Activities

Writing (Guided Reading Teaching Plans, p. 5)

Quick Write (Writing Teacher's Guide, Week 3, p. 91)
Write to Learn (Writing Teacher's Guide, Week 3, p. 91)
***Words Their Way* Connection**
QuickReads® **Connection**

Day 3	Day 4	Day 5
Focus Lesson 2 **Inferring From Visual Sources** (p. 236): *Drums: The World's Heartbeat* 25 minutes **Apply the Strategy** (p. 237) **Informal Assessment** (p. 241): **Behaviors to Notice**, bullet 2 **Check for Understanding**, bullet 2 15 minutes	*Focus Lesson 3* **Evaluating Visual Sources** (p. 238): *Drums: The World's Heartbeat* 25 minutes **Apply the Strategy** (p. 239) **Informal Assessment** (p. 241): **Behaviors to Notice**, bullet 3 **Check for Understanding**, bullets 3 & 4 15 minutes *Mini-lesson* **Nonfiction Text Features** (p. 233) 10 minutes	**Pause and Reflect** (p. 240) 15 minutes **Write About It** (p. 240) 15 minutes
20–30 minutes for each Guided Reading group 10–20 minutes for each Center Activity	20–30 minutes for each Guided Reading group 10–20 minutes for each Center Activity	20–30 minutes for each Guided Reading group 10–20 minutes for each Center Activity
Lesson 3 **Prewriting** (p. 102) 30 minutes **Grammar/Usage Follow-up Activity** (p. 111) 15 minutes	*Lesson 4* **Prewriting** (p. 103) **Informal Assessment** (p. 111): **Reflective Writing**, bullet 3 35 minutes	**Flexible Time** Use this time to have students work on their writing or to focus on an aspect of writing. You may also confer with students or use one of the assessment materials listed below.

Assessment

Shared Reading and Guided Reading

- Have students update their **Reading Log**.
- Use the **Guided Reading Skills Checklist** to keep a record of skills students have acquired from the Guided Reading lessons.

Writing

- Use the **Conference Card** to confer with students.

	Day **1**	Day **2**	
Shared Reading **Unit 5/Week 4**: Great Readers Read to Learn/Identifying and Using Text Structures Teacher's Guide, pp. 242–251 Total time: 30–50 minutes per day	**Introduce the Teacher Modeling Text**: *First-Aid Handbook* 10 minutes **Introduce the Student Reader, Vol. 2**: *Charting Your Course* 10 minutes *Mini-lesson* **Word Study** (p. 243) 10 minutes	*Focus Lesson 1* **Identifying Text Structures** (p. 244): *First-Aid Handbook* 25 minutes **Apply the Strategy** (p. 245) **Informal Assessment** (p. 251): **Behaviors to Notice**, bullet 1 **Check for Understanding**, bullet 1 15 minutes	
Guided Reading/ *Center Activities* Total time: 60 minutes per day	20–30 minutes for each Guided Reading group 10–20 minutes for each Center Activity	20–30 minutes for each Guided Reading group 10–20 minutes for each Center Activity	
Writing **Unit 5/Week 4**: Informational Writing/Science Report Teacher's Guide, pp. 104–107 Total time: 35–45 minutes per day	*Lesson 1* **Trait Time—Sentence Fluency** (p. 104) 30 minutes **Grammar/Usage/Mechanics Mini-lesson** (p. 151) 15 minutes	*Lesson 2* **Drafting** (p. 105) **Informal Assessment** (p. 111): **Reflective Writing**, bullet 4 35 minutes	

Guided Reading

Teaching Plans

DRA Level 40 *Bird-Watching; Clay Magic: The Art of Clay Animation; Diving in Antarctica; The Guitar: King of Strings; Save Our Earth*
DRA Level 34 *Butterflies and Moths; Make It, Wear It*

DRA Level 30 *At Home in the Sea; Koalas; Mailman Mario and His Boris Busters*

Center Activities

Writing (Guided Reading Teaching Plans, p. 5)

Quick Write (Writing Teacher's Guide, Week 4, p. 91)

Write to Learn (Writing Teacher's Guide, Week 4, p. 91)

Words Their Way **Connection**

QuickReads® **Connection**

Day **3**	Day **4**	Day **5**
Focus Lesson 2 **Linking Text Structure and Author's Purpose** (p. 246): *First-Aid Handbook* 25 minutes **Apply the Strategy** (p. 247) **Informal Assessment** (p. 251): **Behaviors to Notice,** bullet 2 **Check for Understanding,** bullet 2 15 minutes	*Focus Lesson 3* **Identifying Multiple Text Structures** (p. 248): *First-Aid Handbook* 25 minutes **Apply the Strategy** (p. 249) **Informal Assessment** (p. 251): **Behaviors to Notice,** bullets 3 & 4 **Check for Understanding,** bullets 3 & 4 15 minutes *Mini-lesson* **Nonfiction Text Features** (p. 243) 10 minutes	**Pause and Reflect** (p. 250) 15 minutes **Write About It** (p. 250) 15 minutes
20–30 minutes for each Guided Reading group 10–20 minutes for each Center Activity	20–30 minutes for each Guided Reading group 10–20 minutes for each Center Activity	20–30 minutes for each Guided Reading group 10–20 minutes for each Center Activity
Lesson 3 **Drafting** (p. 106) **Informal Assessment** (p. 111): **Behaviors to Notice,** bullet 4 30 minutes **Grammar/Usage/Mechanics Follow-up Activity** (p. 111) 15 minutes	*Lesson 4* **Drafting** (p. 107) **Informal Assessment** (p. 111): **Behaviors to Notice,** bullet 3 35 minutes	**Flexible Time** Use this time to have students work on their writing or to focus on an aspect of writing. You may also confer with students or use one of the assessment materials listed below.

Assessment

Shared Reading and Guided Reading

- Use the If/then chart in the **Assessment Card** to identify common student problems and provide support.
- Have students update their **Reading Log.**

- Have students select items to add to their reading portfolio.
- Use the **Portfolio Checklist** to make sure each student's portfolio is organized and up-to-date.
- Review students' **Home Reading Record** to monitor home reading habits and respond to questions or concerns of family members.

Writing

- Use the **Conference Card** and **conference forms** as you discuss students' writing with them.

	Day 1	Day 2
Shared Reading **Unit 5/Week 5**: Great Readers Read to Learn/Evaluating Nonfiction Teacher's Guide, pp. 252–261 Total time: 20–50 minutes per day	**Introduce the Student Reader, Vol. 2**: *Charting Your Course* 10 minutes *Mini-lesson* **Nonfiction Text Features** (p. 253) 10 minutes	*Focus Lesson 1* **Asking Questions About the Author** (p. 254): *First-Aid Handbook* 15 minutes **Apply the Strategy** (p. 255) **Informal Assessment** (p. 261): **Behaviors to Notice**, bullet 1 **Check for Understanding**, bullet 1 15 minutes
Guided Reading/ *Center Activities* Total time: 60 minutes per day	20–30 minutes for each Guided Reading group 10–20 minutes for each Center Activity	20–30 minutes for each Guided Reading group 10–20 minutes for each Center Activity
Writing **Unit 5/Week 5**: Informational Writing/Science Report Teacher's Guide, pp. 108–111 Total time: 35–45 minutes per day	*Lesson 1* **Revising** (p. 108) 30 minutes **Grammar/Usage/Mechanics Mini-lesson** (p. 151) 15 minutes	**Flexible Time** Use this time to have students work on their writing or to focus on an aspect of writing. You may also confer with students or use one of the assessment materials listed below.

Guided Reading

Teaching Plans

DRA Level 40 *The Ancient Ones: The Anasazi of Mesa Verde; Building Bridges; Maya Lin: Linking People and Places; Olympic Champions; Seeing Is Not Believing; Volcanoes*
DRA Level 38 *People of the Canyon; They Changed the World; A Year in Antarctica*

DRA Level 34 *Beetles; Playground Science*
DRA Level 30 *Koalas*

Center Activities

Writing (Guided Reading Teaching Plans, p. 5)

Quick Write (Writing Teacher's Guide, Week 5, p. 91)

Write to Learn (Writing Teacher's Guide, Week 5, p. 91)

Digging Deeper (Writing Teacher's Guide, Week 5, p. 111)

***Words Their Way* Connection**

QuickReads® Connection

Day **3**	Day **4**	Day **5**
Focus Lesson 2 **Evaluating the Authenticity of Information** (p. 256): *First-Aid Handbook* 15 minutes **Apply the Strategy** (p. 257) **Informal Assessment** (p. 261): **Behaviors to Notice,** bullet 2 **Check for Understanding,** bullet 2 15 minutes	*Focus Lesson 3* **Evaluating the Clarity of Information** (p. 258): *First-Aid Handbook* 25 minutes **Apply the Strategy** (p. 259) **Informal Assessment** (p. 261): **Behaviors to Notice,** bullets 3 & 4 **Check for Understanding,** bullets 3 & 4 15 minutes *Mini-lesson* **Word Study** (p. 253) 10 minutes	**Celebrations** (p. 260) 15 minutes **Write About It** (p. 260) 15 minutes
20–30 minutes for each Guided Reading group 10–20 minutes for each Center Activity	20–30 minutes for each Guided Reading group 10–20 minutes for each Center Activity	20–30 minutes for each Guided Reading group 10–20 minutes for each Center Activity
Lesson 2 **Revising** (p. 109) **Informal Assessment** (p. 111): **Reflective Writing,** bullet 5 **Behaviors to Notice,** bullet 5 35 minutes	**Flexible Time** Use this time to have students work on their writing or to focus on an aspect of writing. You may also confer with students or use one of the assessment materials listed below.	*Lesson 3* **Editing** (p. 110) **Informal Assessment** (p. 111): **Reflective Writing,** bullet 2 30 minutes **Grammar/Usage/Mechanics Follow-up Activity** (p. 111) 15 minutes

Assessment

Shared Reading and Guided Reading

- Use the **Checklist of Good Habits, Unit 5,** to assess students' understanding of strategies taught.
- Use the If/then chart in the **Assessment Card** to identify common student problems and provide support.

- Have students update their **Reading Log.**

Writing

- Use the **Conference Card** to confer with students.
- Use the **research report anchor papers** and **rubric** to assess students' science reports.
- Use the **Informational Writing Teacher Evaluation Checklist**

to track students' acquisition of informational writing skills.

- Have students add their science report to their writing portfolio and complete the **portfolio forms.**
- Have students update their **Writing Log.**
- Have students use the **Self-Reflection Form** to self-assess their writing and to set and evaluate goals.

	Day 1	Day 2
Shared Reading **Unit 6/Week 1:** Great Readers Monitor and Organize Ideas and Information/Taking Notes on Fiction Teacher's Guide, pp. 268–277 Total time: 30–40 minutes per day	**Introduce the Teacher Modeling Text:** *The Renaissance Kids* 10 minutes **Introduce the Student Reader, Vol. 3:** *Anna-Maria's Moccasins* 10 minutes *Mini-lesson* **Writer's Craft** (p. 269) 10 minutes	*Focus Lesson 1* **Matching a Graphic Organizer to Text** (p. 270): *The Renaissance Kids* 15 minutes **Apply the Strategy** (p. 271) **Informal Assessment** (p. 277): **Behaviors to Notice,** bullet 1 **Check for Understanding,** bullet 1 15 minutes
Guided Reading/ *Center Activities* Total time: 60 minutes per day	20–30 minutes for each Guided Reading group 10–20 minutes for each Center Activity	20–30 minutes for each Guided Reading group 10–20 minutes for each Center Activity
Writing **Catch-up Week** You may wish to use this week to have students complete unfinished writing projects or do any of the writing activities listed under *Center Activities*.		

Guided Reading

Teaching Plans

DRA Level 40 *Chain Reaction; Green Treasure; Kids in Charge; The Story of Persephone; Trading Places in Timbuktu: A Tale from Mali*
DRA Level 34 *The Plant That Almost Ate the World*
DRA Level 30 *A Day at the Races; Fossil Find; Grasslands*

Center Activities

Writing (Guided Reading Teaching Plans, p. 5)

***Words Their Way* Connection**

***QuickReads*® Connection**

Day 3	Day 4	Day 5
Focus Lesson 2 **Using a Graphic Organizer to Understand the Text** (p. 272): *The Renaissance Kids* 25 minutes **Apply the Strategy** (p. 273) **Informal Assessment** (p. 277): **Behaviors to Notice,** bullet 2 **Check for Understanding,** bullet 2 15 minutes	*Focus Lesson 3* **Using a Graphic Organizer to Evaluate Characters** (p. 274): *The Renaissance Kids* 15 minutes **Apply the Strategy** (p. 275) **Informal Assessment** (p. 277): **Behaviors to Notice,** bullets 3 & 4 **Check for Understanding,** bullets 3 & 4 15 minutes *Mini-lesson* **Fluency** (p. 269) 10 minutes	**Pause and Reflect** (p. 276) 15 minutes **Write About It** (p. 276) 15 minutes
20–30 minutes for each Guided Reading group 10–20 minutes for each Center Activity	20–30 minutes for each Guided Reading group 10–20 minutes for each Center Activity	20–30 minutes for each Guided Reading group 10–20 minutes for each Center Activity

Assessment

Shared Reading and Guided Reading

- Use the **Summary Rubric** to assess students' ability to summarize a fiction or nonfiction text.
- Use the **Running Record** to assess students' comprehension, fluency, and word-solving strategies.

- Use the If/then chart in the **Assessment Card** to identify common student problems and provide support.
- Have students select items to add to their reading portfolio.
- Have students update their **Reading Log**.

- Use the **Guided Reading Discussion Checklist** to assess students' speaking and listening skills during Guided Reading.
- Use the **Guided Reading Skills Checklist** to keep a record of skills students have acquired from the Guided Reading lessons.

	Day 1	Day 2	
Shared Reading **Unit 6/Week 2**: Great Readers Monitor and Organize Ideas and Information/Taking Notes on Nonfiction Teacher's Guide, pp. 278–287 Total time: 30–40 minutes per day	**Introduce the Teacher Modeling Text:** *Blast Zone* 10 minutes **Introduce the Student Reader, Vol. 3:** *Wild and Wacky Festivals* 10 minutes *Mini-lesson* **Writer's Craft** (p. 279) 10 minutes	*Focus Lesson 1* **Matching a Graphic Organizer to Text** (p. 280): *Blast Zone* 25 minutes **Apply the Strategy** (p. 281) **Informal Assessment** (p. 287): **Behaviors to Notice,** bullet 1 **Check for Understanding,** bullet 1 15 minutes	
Guided Reading/ *Center Activities* Total time: 60 minutes per day	20–30 minutes for each Guided Reading group 10–20 minutes for each Center Activity	20–30 minutes for each Guided Reading group 10–20 minutes for each Center Activity	
Writing * **Unit 6/Week 1:** Writing to Explain and Learn/News Story Teacher's Guide, pp. 112–117 Total time: 35–45 minutes per day * Please note that the Writing Week number is different from the Shared Reading Week number.	*Lesson 1* **Prewriting** (p. 114) 30 minutes **Grammar/Usage Mini-lesson** (p. 152) 15 minutes	*Lesson 2* **Drafting** (p. 115) 35 minutes	

Guided Reading

Teaching Plans

DRA Level 40 *Amazing Arachnids; Diving in Antarctica; The Living Desert; Save Our Earth; Stop Here! Remarkable Roadside Attractions*
DRA Level 38 *Encyclopedia of World Sports; Shark Attack!; Water Wise*
DRA Level 34 *Introducing Snakes*
DRA Level 30 *A Day at the Races*

Center Activities

Writing (Guided Reading Teaching Plans, p. 5)
Quick Write (Writing Teacher's Guide, Week 1, p. 113)
Write to Learn (Writing Teacher's Guide, Week 1, p. 113)

***Words Their Way* Connection**
QuickReads® **Connection**

Day 3	Day 4	Day 5
Focus Lesson 2 **Using a Graphic Organizer to Understand the Text** (p. 282): *Blast Zone* 25 minutes **Apply the Strategy** (p. 283) **Informal Assessment** (p. 287): **Behaviors to Notice,** bullets 2–5 **Check for Understanding,** bullet 2 15 minutes	*Focus Lesson 3* **Using a Graphic Organizer as an Aid to Retelling/Summarizing** (p. 284): *Blast Zone* 15 minutes **Apply the Strategy** (p. 285) **Informal Assessment** (p. 287): **Check for Understanding,** bullets 3 & 4 15 minutes *Mini-lesson* **Fluency** (p. 279) 10 minutes	**Pause and Reflect** (p. 286) 15 minutes **Write About It** (p. 286) 15 minutes
20–30 minutes for each Guided Reading group 10–20 minutes for each Center Activity	20–30 minutes for each Guided Reading group 10–20 minutes for each Center Activity	20–30 minutes for each Guided Reading group 10–20 minutes for each Center Activity
Flexible Time Use this time to have students work on their writing or to focus on an aspect of writing. You may also confer with students or use one of the assessment materials listed below.	*Lesson 3* **Drafting** (p. 116) 30 minutes **Grammar/Usage Follow-up Activity** (p. 127) 15 minutes	*Lesson 4* **Revising** (p. 117) **Informal Assessment** (p. 126): **Reflective Writing,** bullets 1 & 2 **Behaviors to Notice,** bullets 2 & 5 35 minutes

Assessment

Shared Reading and Guided Reading

- Use the **Independent Reading Behaviors Checklist** to assess students' ability to select, read, and comprehend text independently.
- Use the If/then chart in the **Assessment Card** to identify common student problems and provide support.

- Have students update their **Reading Log.**

Writing

- Use the **Conference Card** and **conference forms** as you discuss students' writing with them.
- Have students add their news story to their writing portfolio and complete the **portfolio forms.**

	Day **1**	Day **2**	
Shared Reading **Unit 6/Week 3**: Great Readers Monitor and Organize Ideas and Information/Self-Monitoring Teacher's Guide, pp. 288–297 Total time: 20–40 minutes per day	**Introduce the Student Reader, Vol. 3**: *Friends in the Sea* 10 minutes *Mini-lesson* **Fluency** (p. 289) 10 minutes	*Focus Lesson 1* **Pausing to Monitor Comprehension** (p. 290): *Blast Zone* 25 minutes **Apply the Strategy** (p. 291) **Informal Assessment** (p. 297): **Behaviors to Notice**, bullet 1 **Check for Understanding**, bullets 2 & 3 15 minutes	
Guided Reading/ *Center Activities* Total time: 60 minutes per day	20–30 minutes for each Guided Reading group 10–20 minutes for each Center Activity	20–30 minutes for each Guided Reading group 10–20 minutes for each Center Activity	
Writing * **Unit 6/Week 2**: Writing to Explain and Learn/How-To Essay Teacher's Guide, pp. 118–121 Total time: 35–45 minutes per day * Please note that the Writing Week number is different from the Shared Reading Week number.	*Lesson 1* **Prewriting** (p. 118) 30 minutes **Grammar/Usage/Mechanics Mini-lesson** (p. 152) 15 minutes	*Lesson 2* **Drafting** (p. 119) **Informal Assessment** (p. 126): **Behaviors to Notice**, bullet 3 35 minutes	

Guided Reading

Teaching Plans

DRA Level 40 *Building Bridges; Louisa, the Blind Kitten; North to the Pole With Matthew Henson; Nutty for Peanuts*
DRA Level 38 *The Adventures of Robin Hood; People of the Canyon*
DRA Level 34 *The Mystery of the Spy's Diary*
DRA Level 30 *At Home on a Coral Reef*

Center Activities

Writing (Guided Reading Teaching Plans, p. 5)

Quick Write (Writing Teacher's Guide, Week 2, p. 113)

Write to Learn (Writing Teacher's Guide, Week 2, p. 113)

***Words Their Way* Connection**

QuickReads® Connection

Day 3	Day 4	Day 5
Focus Lesson 2 **Rereading to Regain Meaning** (p. 292): *Blast Zone* 25 minutes **Apply the Strategy** (p. 293) **Informal Assessment** (p. 297): **Behaviors to Notice**, bullet 2 **Check for Understanding,** bullets 1 & 4 15 minutes	*Focus Lesson 3* **Sequencing Ideas to Regain Meaning** (p. 294): *Blast Zone* 15 minutes **Apply the Strategy** (p. 295) **Informal Assessment** (p. 297): **Behaviors to Notice**, bullet 3 **Check for Understanding**, bullet 5 15 minutes *Mini-lesson* **Nonfiction Text Features** (p. 289) 10 minutes	**Pause and Reflect** (p. 296) 15 minutes **Write About It** (p. 296) 15 minutes
20–30 minutes for each Guided Reading group 10–20 minutes for each Center Activity	20–30 minutes for each Guided Reading group 10–20 minutes for each Center Activity	20–30 minutes for each Guided Reading group 10–20 minutes for each Center Activity
Lesson 3 **Drafting** (p. 120) 30 minutes **Grammar/Usage/Mechanics Follow-up Activity** (p. 127) 15 minutes	**Flexible Time** Use this time to have students work on their writing or to focus on an aspect of writing. You may also confer with students or use one of the assessment materials listed below.	*Lesson 4* **Revising** (p. 121) **Informal Assessment** (p. 126): **Reflective Writing,** bullet 3 35 minutes

Assessment

Shared Reading and Guided Reading

- Have students update their **Reading Log**.
- Have students select items to add to their reading portfolio.
- Use the **Portfolio Checklist** to make sure each student's portfolio is organized and up-to-date.

- Use the **Text Frame** to support students' written retelling of a nonfiction selection.

Writing

- Use the **Conference Card** to confer with students.
- Have students add their how-to essay to their writing portfolio and complete the **portfolio forms**.

	Day **1**	Day **2**
Shared Reading **Unit 6/Week 4**: Great Readers Monitor and Organize Ideas and Information/Visualizing Teacher's Guide, pp. 298–307 Total time: 20–40 minutes per day	**Introduce the Student Reader, Vol. 3**: *Friends in the Sea* 10 minutes *Mini-lesson* **Writer's Craft** (p. 299) 10 minutes	*Focus Lesson 1* **Using Background Knowledge and Text to Visualize** (p. 300): *Blast Zone* 25 minutes **Apply the Strategy** (p. 301) **Informal Assessment** (p. 307): **Behaviors to Notice**, bullets 1 & 2 15 minutes
Guided Reading/ *Center Activities* Total time: 60 minutes per day	20–30 minutes for each Guided Reading group 10–20 minutes for each Center Activity	20–30 minutes for each Guided Reading group 10–20 minutes for each Center Activity
Writing * **Unit 6/Week 3**: Writing to Explain and Learn/Journal Entry Teacher's Guide, pp. 122–127 Total time: 35–45 minutes per day * Please note that the Writing Week number is different from the Shared Reading Week number.	*Lesson 1* **Prewriting** (p. 122) **Informal Assessment** (p. 126): **Behaviors to Notice**, bullet 1 30 minutes **Grammar/Usage Mini-lesson** (p. 152) 15 minutes	*Lesson 2* **Prewriting** (p. 123) 35 minutes

Guided Reading

Teaching Plans

DRA Level 40 *The Great Bamboozle; Robots*
DRA Level 38 *Tikky, Tikky Spider*

Center Activities

Writing (Guided Reading Teaching Plans, p. 5)

Quick Write (Writing Teacher's Guide, Week 3, p. 113)

Write to Learn (Writing Teacher's Guide, Week 3, p. 113)

***Words Their Way* Connection**

***QuickReads*® Connection**

Day 3

Focus Lesson 2
Using Descriptive Phrases to Create Mental and Sensory Images (p. 302): *Blast Zone*
25 minutes

Apply the Strategy (p. 303)
Informal Assessment (p. 307):
Behaviors to Notice, bullet 3
Check for Understanding, bullet 2
15 minutes

20–30 minutes for each Guided Reading group

10–20 minutes for each Center Activity

Lesson 3
Drafting (p. 124)
30 minutes

Grammar/Usage Follow-up Activity (p. 127)
15 minutes

Day 4

Focus Lesson 3
Modifying Visualizations as You Read (p. 304): *Blast Zone*
15 minutes

Apply the Strategy (p. 305)
Informal Assessment (p. 307):
Behaviors to Notice, bullet 4
Check for Understanding, bullets 1, 3, & 4
15 minutes

Mini-lesson
Nonfiction Structure (p. 299)
10 minutes

20–30 minutes for each Guided Reading group

10–20 minutes for each Center Activity

Flexible Time Use this time to have students work on their writing or to focus on an aspect of writing. You may also confer with students or use one of the assessment materials listed below.

Day 5

Celebrations (p. 306)
15 minutes

Write About It (p. 306)
15 minutes

20–30 minutes for each Guided Reading group

10–20 minutes for each Center Activity

Lesson 4
Revising (p. 125)
Informal Assessment (p. 126):
Reflective Writing, bullet 4
Behaviors to Notice, bullet 4
35 minutes

Assessment

Shared Reading and Guided Reading

- Use the **Checklist of Good Habits, Unit 6**, to assess students' understanding of strategies taught.
- Use the **Assessment Card** to help determine if students are ready to move to the next reading level.
- Have students update their **Reading Log**.

- Use the **Guided Reading Skills Checklist** to keep a record of skills students have acquired from the Guided Reading lessons.
- Review students' **Home Reading Record** to monitor home reading habits and respond to questions or concerns of family members.

Writing

- Use the **Conference Card** to confer with students.

- Have students add their journal entry to their writing portfolio and complete the **portfolio forms**.
- Have students update their **Writing Log**.
- Have students use the **Self-Reflection Form** to self-assess their writing and to set and evaluate goals.

	Day 1	Day 2
Shared Reading **Unit 7/Week 1:** Great Readers Think Critically About Books/ Questioning the Commonplace in a Text Teacher's Guide, pp. 314–323 Total time: 30–40 minutes per day	**Introduce the Teacher Modeling Text:** *Hare Rescues the Sun and Other Sky Myths* 10 minutes **Introduce the Student Reader, Vol. 3:** *Little Bear and Other Native American Animal Tales* 10 minutes *Mini-lesson* **Fluency** (p. 315) 10 minutes	*Focus Lesson 1* **Questioning the Archetype of Heroes and Villains** (p. 316): *Hare Rescues the Sun and Other Sky Myths* 15 minutes **Apply the Strategy** (p. 317) **Informal Assessment** (p. 323): **Behaviors to Notice**, bullet 1 **Check for Understanding**, bullet 1 15 minutes
Guided Reading/ *Center Activities* Total time: 60 minutes per day	20–30 minutes for each Guided Reading group 10–20 minutes for each Center Activity	20–30 minutes for each Guided Reading group 10–20 minutes for each Center Activity
Writing **Unit 7/Week 1:** Persuasive Writing/Letter to the Editor Teacher's Guide, pp. 128–133 Total time: 35–45 minutes per day	*Lesson 1* **Prewriting** (p. 130) **Informal Assessment** (p. 145): **Behaviors to Notice,** bullets 1 & 2 30 minutes **Grammar/Usage/Mechanics Mini-lesson** (p. 153) 15 minutes	*Lesson 2* **Prewriting** (p. 131) 35 minutes

Guided Reading

Teaching Plans

DRA Level 40 *Trading Places in Timbuktu: A Tale from Mali; What's the Fashion?*
DRA Level 34 *Amphibians; Looking at Lizards*

Center Activities

Writing (Guided Reading Teaching Plans, p. 5)
Quick Write (Writing Teacher's Guide, Week 1, p. 129)
Write to Learn (Writing Teacher's Guide, Week 1, p. 129)

***Words Their Way* Connection**
***QuickReads*® Connection**

Day 3	Day 4	Day 5
Focus Lesson 2 **Considering the Role of Gender** (p. 318): *Hare Rescues the Sun and Other Sky Myths* 15 minutes **Apply the Strategy** (p. 319) **Informal Assessment** (p. 323): **Behaviors to Notice,** bullet 2 **Check for Understanding,** bullet 2 15 minutes	*Focus Lesson 3* **Considering the Role of Wealth and Class** (p. 320): *Hare Rescues the Sun and Other Sky Myths* 15 minutes **Apply the Strategy** (p. 321) **Informal Assessment** (p. 323): **Behaviors to Notice,** bullet 3 **Check for Understanding,** bullets 3 & 4 15 minutes *Mini-lesson* **Word Study** (p. 315) 10 minutes	**Pause and Reflect** (p. 322) 15 minutes **Write About It** (p. 322) 15 minutes
20–30 minutes for each Guided Reading group **10–20 minutes** for each Center Activity	**20–30 minutes** for each Guided Reading group **10–20 minutes** for each Center Activity	**20–30 minutes** for each Guided Reading group **10–20 minutes** for each Center Activity
Lesson 3 **Prewriting** (p. 132) **Informal Assessment** **Behaviors to Notice,** bullet 4 30 minutes **Grammar/Usage/Mechanics Follow-up Activity** (p. 145) 15 minutes	*Lesson 4* **Prewriting** (p. 133) 35 minutes	**Flexible Time** Use this time to have students work on their writing or to focus on an aspect of writing. You may also confer with students or use one of the assessment materials listed below.

Assessment

Shared Reading and Guided Reading

- Use the If/then chart in the **Assessment Card** to identify common student problems and provide support.
- Have students select items to add to their reading portfolio.

- Have students update their **Reading Log.**
- Use the **Guided Reading Skills Checklist** to keep a record of skills students have acquired from the Guided Reading lessons.

Writing

- Use the **Conference Card** to confer with students.

	Day 1	Day 2
Shared Reading **Unit 7/Week 2**: Great Readers Think Critically About Books/ Considering the Role of the Author Teacher's Guide, pp. 324–333 Total time: 20–50 minutes per day	**Introduce the Student Reader, Vol. 3:** *Little Bear and Other Native American Animal Tales* 10 minutes *Mini-lesson* **Writer's Craft** (p. 325) 10 minutes	*Focus Lesson 1* **Thinking About the Author's Sources of Information** (p. 326): *Hare Rescues the Sun and Other Sky Myths* 25 minutes **Apply the Strategy** (p. 327) **Informal Assessment** (p. 333): **Behaviors to Notice**, bullet 1 **Check for Understanding**, bullet 1 15 minutes
Guided Reading/ *Center Activities* Total time: 60 minutes per day	20–30 minutes for each Guided Reading group 10–20 minutes for each Center Activity	20–30 minutes for each Guided Reading group 10–20 minutes for each Center Activity
Writing **Unit 7/Week 2**: Persuasive Writing/Letter to the Editor Teacher's Guide, pp. 134–137 Total time: 35–45 minutes per day	*Lesson 1* **Trait Time—Conventions** (p. 134) 30 minutes **Grammar/Usage Mini-lesson** (p. 153) 15 minutes	*Lesson 2* **Drafting** (p. 135) 35 minutes

Guided Reading

Teaching Plans

DRA Level 40 *African American Cowboys: True Heroes of the Old West; Chain Reaction; Diving in Antarctica; Trading Places in Timbuktu: A Tale from Mali*
DRA Level 38 *Water Wise; ZD3, The Handy Robot*

DRA Level 30 *Fossil Find; Who Works in a Hospital?*

Center Activities

Writing (Guided Reading Teaching Plans, p. 5)
Quick Write (Writing Teacher's Guide, Week 2, p. 129)

Write to Learn (Writing Teacher's Guide, Week 2, p. 129)
Digging Deeper (Writing Teacher's Guide, Week 2, p. 145)
***Words Their Way* Connection**
QuickReads® **Connection**

Day 3	Day 4	Day 5
Focus Lesson 2 **Considering the Author's Motives** (p. 328): *Hare Rescues the Sun and Other Sky Myths* 15 minutes **Apply the Strategy** (p. 329) **Informal Assessment** (p. 333): **Behaviors to Notice**, bullet 2 **Check for Understanding**, bullet 2 15 minutes	*Focus Lesson 3* **Recognizing That Characters Represent the Author's Message** (p. 330): *Hare Rescues the Sun and Other Sky Myths* 25 minutes **Apply the Strategy** (p. 331) **Informal Assessment** (p. 333): **Behaviors to Notice**, bullet 3 **Check for Understanding**, bullets 3 & 4 15 minutes *Mini-lesson* **Word Study** (p. 325) 10 minutes	**Pause and Reflect** (p. 332) 15 minutes **Write About It** (p. 332) 15 minutes
20–30 minutes for each Guided Reading group 10–20 minutes for each Center Activity	20–30 minutes for each Guided Reading group 10–20 minutes for each Center Activity	20–30 minutes for each Guided Reading group 10–20 minutes for each Center Activity
Lesson 3 **Drafting** (p. 136) **Informal Assessment** (p. 145): **Behaviors to Notice**, bullet 3 30 minutes **Grammar/Usage Follow-up Activity** (p. 145) 15 minutes	**Flexible Time** Use this time to have students work on their writing or to focus on an aspect of writing. You may also confer with students or use one of the assessment materials listed below.	*Lesson 4* **Drafting** (p. 137) **Informal Assessment** (p. 145): **Reflective Writing**, bullet 1 35 minutes

Assessment

Shared Reading and Guided Reading

- Use the If/then chart in the **Assessment Card** to identify common student problems and provide support.
- Use the **Running Record** to assess students' comprehension.

- Have students update their **Reading Log**.
- Use the **Guided Reading Discussion Checklist** to assess students' speaking and listening skills during Guided Reading.

- Use the **Guided Reading Skills Checklist** to keep a record of skills students have acquired from the Guided Reading lessons.

Writing

- Use the **Conference Card** and **conference forms** as you discuss students' writing with them.

Week 3 DAILY PLANNER

	Day 1	Day 2	
Shared Reading **Unit 7/Week 3:** Great Readers Think Critically About Books/ Seeking Alternative Perspectives Teacher's Guide, pp. 334–343 Total time: 30–50 minutes per day	**Introduce the Teacher Modeling Text:** *The Renaissance Kids* 10 minutes **Introduce the Student Reader, Vol. 3:** *Three Cheers for Planet Earth; Saving the Florida Panther* 10 minutes *Mini-lesson* **Word Study** (p. 335) 10 minutes	*Focus Lesson 1* **Identifying Other Perspectives on a Topic** (p. 336): *The Renaissance Kids* 15 minutes **Apply the Strategy** (p. 337) **Informal Assessment** (p. 343): **Behaviors to Notice,** bullet 1 **Check for Understanding,** bullet 1 15 minutes	
Guided Reading/ *Center Activities* Total time: 60 minutes per day	20–30 minutes for each Guided Reading group 10–20 minutes for each Center Activity	20–30 minutes for each Guided Reading group 10–20 minutes for each Center Activity	
Writing **Unit 7/Week 3:** Persuasive Writing/Letter to the Editor Teacher's Guide, pp. 138–140 Total time: 35–45 minutes per day	*Lesson 1* **Revising** (p. 138) 30 minutes **Grammar/Usage/Mechanics Mini-lesson** (p. 153) 15 minutes	**Flexible Time** Use this time to have students work on their writing or to focus on an aspect of writing. You may also confer with students or use one of the assessment materials listed below.	

Guided Reading

Teaching Plans

DRA Level 40 *African American Cowboys: True Heroes of the Old West; The Ancient Ones: The Anasazi of Mesa Verde; Crossing Borders: Stories of Immigrants*
DRA Level 38 *The Creature Vanishes; A Year in Antarctica*
DRA Level 34 *The San Francisco Exploratorium*

Center Activities

Writing (Guided Reading Teaching Plans, p. 5)
Quick Write (Writing Teacher's Guide, Week 3, p. 129)
Write to Learn (Writing Teacher's Guide, Week 3, p. 129)

***Words Their Way* Connection**
QuickReads® Connection

Day 3	Day 4	Day 5
Focus Lesson 2 **Considering Historical and Cultural Influences on a Text** (p. 338): *The Renaissance Kids* 25 minutes **Apply the Strategy** (p. 339) **Informal Assessment** (p. 343): **Behaviors to Notice**, bullet 2 **Check for Understanding**, bullet 2 15 minutes	*Focus Lesson 3* **Comparing Other Perspectives Between Texts** (p. 340): *The Renaissance Kids*; William Shakespeare article 25 minutes **Apply the Strategy** (p. 341) **Informal Assessment** (p. 343): **Behaviors to Notice**, bullet 3 **Check for Understanding**, bullets 3 & 4 15 minutes *Mini-lesson* **Nonfiction Text Features** (p. 335) 10 minutes	**Pause and Reflect** (p. 342) 15 minutes **Write About It** (p. 342) 15 minutes
20–30 minutes for each Guided Reading group 10–20 minutes for each Center Activity	20–30 minutes for each Guided Reading group 10–20 minutes for each Center Activity	20–30 minutes for each Guided Reading group 10–20 minutes for each Center Activity
Lesson 2 **Revising** (p. 139) **Informal Assessment** (p. 145): **Reflective Writing**, bullets 2 & 3 35 minutes	**Flexible Time** Use this time to have students work on their writing or to focus on an aspect of writing. You may also confer with students or use one of the assessment materials listed below.	*Lesson 3* **Editing** (p. 140) 30 minutes **Grammar/Usage/Mechanics Follow-up Activity** (p. 145) 15 minutes

Assessment

Shared Reading and Guided Reading

- Use the **Summary Rubric** to assess students' ability to summarize a fiction or nonfiction text.
- Use the If/then chart in the **Assessment Card** to identify common student problems and provide support.

- Have students update their **Reading Log**.
- Have students select items to add to their reading portfolio.
- Use the **Portfolio Checklist** to make sure each student's portfolio is organized and up-to-date.

Writing

- Use the **Conference Card** to confer with students.
- Use the **persuasive letter anchor papers** and **rubric** to assess students' letters.
- Have students add their letter to their writing portfolio and complete the **portfolio forms**.

	Day 1	Day 2	
Shared Reading **Unit 7/Week 4**: Great Readers Think Critically About Books/Reading Critically Teacher's Guide, pp. 344–353 Total time: 30–50 minutes per day	**Introduce the Teacher Modeling Text:** *It Can Be Done!: The Life and Legacy of César Chávez* 10 minutes **Introduce the Student Reader, Vol. 3:** *Making Connections: American Indians and Settlers* 10 minutes *Mini-lesson* **Word Study** (p. 345) 10 minutes	*Focus Lesson 1* **Recognizing Bias** (p. 346): *It Can Be Done!: The Life and Legacy of César Chávez* 25 minutes **Apply the Strategy** (p. 347) **Informal Assessment** (p. 353): **Behaviors to Notice,** bullets 1 & 2 **Check for Understanding,** bullet 1 15 minutes	
Guided Reading/ *Center Activities* Total time: 60 minutes per day	20–30 minutes for each Guided Reading group 10–20 minutes for each Center Activity	20–30 minutes for each Guided Reading group 10–20 minutes for each Center Activity	
Writing **Unit 7/Week 4**: Persuasive Writing/Persuasive Poster Teacher's Guide, pp. 141–145 Total time: 35–45 minutes per day	*Lesson 1* **Prewriting** (p. 141) 30 minutes **Grammar/Usage Mini-lesson** (p. 153) 15 minutes	*Lesson 2* **Prewriting** (p. 142) 35 minutes	

Guided Reading

Teaching Plans

DRA Level 40 *African American Cowboys: True Heroes of the Old West; Crossing Borders: Stories of Immigrants; Wacky Weather; What's the Fashion?; What's That Date Again?*
DRA Level 38 *Chasing Tornados*
DRA Level 34 *Amphibians; First Kids*

DRA Level 30 *The Great Riddle Mystery; Secrets of the Rainforest*

Center Activities

Writing (Guided Reading Teaching Plans, p. 5)

Quick Write (Writing Teacher's Guide, Week 4, p. 129)

Write to Learn (Writing Teacher's Guide, Week 4, p. 129)

***Words Their Way* Connection**
QuickReads® **Connection**

Day 3

Focus Lesson 2
Recognizing What Might Be Missing From the Text (p. 348): *It Can Be Done!: The Life and Legacy of César Chávez*
25 minutes

Apply the Strategy (p. 349)
Informal Assessment (p. 353):
Behaviors to Notice, bullet 3
Check for Understanding, bullet 2
15 minutes

20–30 minutes for each Guided Reading group

10–20 minutes for each Center Activity

Lesson 3
Drafting (p. 143)
30 minutes

Grammar/Usage Follow-up Activity (p. 145)
15 minutes

Day 4

Focus Lesson 3
Making and Supporting Value Judgments (p. 350): *It Can Be Done!: The Life and Legacy of César Chávez*
25 minutes

Apply the Strategy (p. 351)
Informal Assessment (p. 353):
Behaviors to Notice, bullet 4
Check for Understanding, bullets 3–5
15 minutes

Mini-lesson
Fluency (p. 345)
10 minutes

20–30 minutes for each Guided Reading group

10–20 minutes for each Center Activity

Flexible Time Use this time to have students work on their writing or to focus on an aspect of writing. You may also confer with students or use one of the assessment materials listed below.

Day 5

Celebrations (p. 352)
15 minutes

Write About It (p. 352)
15 minutes

20–30 minutes for each Guided Reading group

10–20 minutes for each Center Activity

Lesson 4
Revising (p. 144)
Informal Assessment (p. 145):
Reflective Writing, bullet 4
Behaviors to Notice, bullets 5 & 6
35 minutes

Assessment

Shared Reading and Guided Reading

- Use the **Checklist of Good Habits, Unit 7,** to assess students' understanding of strategies taught.
- Have students update their **Reading Log.**
- Use the **Independent Reading Behaviors Checklist** to assess students' ability to select,

read, and comprehend text independently.

- Review students' **Home Reading Record** to monitor home reading habits and respond to questions or concerns of family members.

Writing

- Use the **Conference Card** to confer with students.

- Use the **Persuasive Writing Teacher Evaluation Checklist** to assess students' acquisition of persuasive writing skills.
- Have students add their persuasive poster to their writing portfolio and complete the **portfolio forms.**
- Have students update their **Writing Log.**
- Have students complete the **End-of-Year Writing Survey.**